A HAY MAN'S TALE

A HAY MAN'S TALE

The BIOGRAPHY AND HISTORY OF W. J. SMALL

AND THE W. J. SMALL COMPANIES

Judy Small Weitekamp

Library of Congress Control Number: 2006935115

ISBN–13: 978-0-9788879-0-2
ISBN–10: 0-9788879-0-5

A HAY MAN'S TALE
The Biography and History of W. J. Small
and The W. J. Small Companies

First Edition

10 9 8 7 6 5 4 3 2 1

Published by
The MO Group, Safety Harbor, FL

Printed in the United States.

Jacket design by Shane P. Brisson
Interior design by Martin Richardson
Edited by Robert Yehling and Martin Richardson

Contact the MO Group by telephone on 727-692-8019
www.mogbooks.com

This book is dedicated to past employees of The W. J. Small Company

ACKNOWLEDGMENTS

My thanks to family and past employees of W. J. Small who enthusiastically donated most of the information in this book through interviews, photographs and their collective remembrances of Mr. Small and his companies.

Of special help through long interviews were Robert and Beverly Blackwell, Marie Clegg, John Clifton, Jr., Roy Failor, Glenn Hill (deceased), Lucille Jensen Newkirk, Gene O'Dell (deceased), Rodger Shinn, Adrin Small, Harold Small, Kathleen and Elmer Small (both deceased), Bill Wagar (deceased), and last, but not least, Rollin Vandever, who kept after me for years to complete a book about W. J. Small. Without Rollin Vandever's encouragement, I may not have completed this project. A push to begin this writing was Don Seideman, formerly of Neosho, Missouri. Photographs and news articles were collected from family members, Cheryl and Daryl Wilmoth, Sidna Small, my brother, Tom Small, and Mike and Carol Wagar; and from librarians and museum employees in Fredonia and Neodesha, Kansas.

My thanks also to friends and family who read and helped edit this book.

"If we make no other footprints on the sands of time, I should like to feel that our company has contributed some share to the general prosperity of agriculture by this endeavor."

— W. J. Small.
An excerpt from an industry
association speech given in 1945

Contents

W. J. Small.

Preface

W. J. Small was a pioneer in the business of dehydrating alfalfa, one of the most important ingredients in feed for farm animals. His company began in a farm community in the early 1930s. Twenty years later, his products were in demand nationwide.

The W. J. Small Company extended its territory into several states, and its dehydrated alfalfa was sold worldwide. The company had eight divisions, including harvesting, storage, laboratory testing, and sales. It worked in a nearly self-sufficient, independent way, from making its own machinery to printing many of its own business forms.

W. J. ran the business almost single handedly, but the people who worked for him made the company successful. In the 1930s, W. J.'s employees were people confronted by severe economic hardships and were thankful to have jobs under any conditions. The 1940s war years brought more work hours because of employee shortages. Then the employees' greatest challenge was to maintain production. Stories from those loyal W. J. Small Company employees paint a fascinating picture of a different era.

W. J. evolved new methods of preserving alfalfa and pioneered other W. J. Small companies, including Airosol and American Chlorophyll. The W. J. Small companies made a considerable amount of money, and W. J. and his wife, Hazel, true philanthropists, gave time, love, work and money back to their communities' churches, hospitals, Boy Scouts, needy families, and schools.

This history of W. J. Small and his companies is written to recognize W. J. Small and his employees for their contributions to United States agriculture and to the economic stability and wartime security of the nation. It is hoped this tribute will also inspire the subsequent generations who have benefited by these endeavors.

Alfalfa

What is the crop that always pays,
And will mature in forty days;
Resisting drought, the frost, the heat;
Whose roots reach down one hundred feet?
Alfalfa!

What grows in loam, in clay or sand?
What lifts the mortgage off the land?
What crop is cut six times a year
And no foul weeds in it appear?
Alfalfa!

What makes the swine so healthy feel,
And never raise a hungry squeal;
The wholesome food that never fails
To put three curls into their tails?
Alfalfa!

What makes all other stock look nice,
And brings the highest market price?
What fills the milk pails, feeds the calf,
And makes the old cow almost laugh?
Alfalfa!

From a Lexington, Nebraska, newspaper in 1914
– years before man's full understanding of vitamins.

About Alfalfa

Introduction

Alfalfa is a legume. It is neither a grass nor a grain. It has to be planted, but unlike other field crops, it is perennial; planted one year, it voluntarily reappears the next.

Although its seeds are delicate, newly planted alfalfa can last five to six years, and produce up to six cuttings over a period of nine months from March to November. After being cut, alfalfa sprouts new stems alongside the main stem to produce a new crop every six to eight weeks until winter. Under cold or freezing weather conditions, alfalfa lies dormant, storing carbohydrates as energy for new growth in the spring. Its nutritional value is in its leaves, a storehouse of vitamins and minerals. Alfalfa provides the best yields where moisture and sunshine are plentiful, but it is better adapted to irrigated districts and to sub-humid regions than to the more humid or arid localities.

Alfalfa is valuable for crop rotation, leaving the soil rich and productive. It actually builds up fertility of the soil while other crops create erosion and burn up organic content of the soil.

Printed records show that alfalfa was grown agriculturally in Europe, for feeding animals, as early as the 1500s. It is believed to have originated in Asia before 700 B.C. and first cultivated in what is now Iran by Ancient Persians who called it "alfalfach" – "best fodder." Greek and Roman writers of ensuing centuries described it as "an herb that nourishes horses best."

In the 6th century A.D., Chinese herbalists began giving their patients alfalfa to treat kidney stones and to relieve fluid retention and swelling.

Alfalfa made its way to the United States during the California Gold Rush when it was imported from South America. The crops spread to the Midwest where they gained popularity, in no small part, due to the activities of W. J. Small – the subject of this book.

Besides being very palatable, alfalfa contains calcium, magnesium, phosphorus and potassium, plus all known vitamins. It contains several saponins, flavonoids, alkaloids, and eight essential amino acids. It is useful as a treatment for urinary tract infections and kidney, bladder and prostrate disorders while promoting pituitary gland function.

Livestock, sometimes finicky eaters, love alfalfa. Farm animals are attracted to alfalfa in any form it is offered to them – growing in the field, chopped, stacked, shredded or baled. Somewhat like clover, green and sweet smelling with small purple flowers, alfalfa has been referred to as the Queen of Legumes.

Alfalfa is a basic ingredient in most formula feeds. When added to formula feeds, it has been referred to as "the wonder ingredient." Studies show that when fed alfalfa, dairy cattle produce more milk, and beef cattle grow faster. The results of better nutrition show up in breeding animals with stronger and more numerous offspring, shinier coats and less infection and disease.

At one time, alfalfa was used only for its protein and carotene. Carotene is the vegetable form of Vitamin A, the growth vitamin. Carotene is also a known agent that helps prevent heart disease and cancer. Vitamin A, which is necessary for normal life, does not exist in plants in the pure form, but all farm animals can convert carotene into Vitamin A. Common farm grains such as wheat, rye, barley, oats and white corn are practically devoid of carotene. The common method of getting Vitamin A and other nutritional elements into the diet is by the grazing of green pastures in the summer and the feeding of good hay in the winter. Rich summer pasture may provide a store of Vitamin A in the tissues of the animal. When summer pasture is short, feeding alfalfa is a good way of supplying carotene.

Some Family History

Left to right: Wright, Baby Elmer, Jacob, Grace, Gertrude, Lou Ella and Emery.

Wright J. Small was born the second child of Jacob B. Small and Lou Ella M. Eversole. He lived from 1890 to 1981.

Jacob Small, Wright's father, was born in Shelby County, Illinois, July 15, 1860. Wright's mother, Lou Ella, was born September 13, 1863, in Lancaster, *Ohio. Both were from large families; Lou Ella had nine brothers and sisters, and Jacob was the first-born in a family of nine children.*

When Lou Ella was about ten years old, she and her family traveled with a caravan of covered wagons from central

Chapter 1

Ohio, across Indiana to Illinois. They settled in Shelby County. Jacob and Lou Ella were married in Shelbyville, Illinois, on February 14, 1886.

Jacob and Lou Ella had eight children, two of whom died in infancy. Surviving were Emery, Wright, Gertrude, Grace, Elmer and Ora. The first four of these children were born in Illinois; Emery, Wright, Gertrude and Grace, in 1887, 1890, 1892 and 1898. Jacob and Lou Ella moved the family to Rock Island, Texas, in 1898 soon after Grace was born. Wright was eight. Elmer and Ora were born in Rock Island in 1902 and 1907. The Smalls settled in Texas for 13 years.

ROCK ISLAND, TEXAS

When the Smalls lived in Rock Island, it was a small town with a railroad depot, a church-school house and seven or eight buildings that included

The Smalls pose outside their Rock Island home. Left to right: Gertrude, Grace, Lou Ella, Ora, Jacob and Elmer.

the bank, post office, drug store, grocery store and lumberyard.

The family was poor. Gertrude (Gertie), who was six when they moved to Texas, later talked about those days in Rock Island: "We had a hard time down there. Everyone in the family had to work. When we would go home from

Before (above) and after (below) pictures of Rock Island show the devastation caused by a hurricane and its 120 mile-per-hour winds which killed 41 people in July, 1909.

school at night, why, we knew we had to go to the truck garden and cut cabbage or pick strawberries or something to make a living."

Jacob was strict with the children. Elmer later said they never learned to play because they worked all the time. Elmer remembered being beaten by his father once for stopping on his way home from school to play ball with classmates. Elmer, Wright and their brothers sold milk door-to-door, and Jacob sold meat from a one-horse cart. In addition to hand-milking 27 cows every day, Jacob slaughtered and cured the beef he raised.

Wright and his siblings grew up in horse-and-buggy days. There were no telephones or radios in the house, and the children studied by coal oil lamps. The children went to Rock Island's public school which was also the church. It was a one-room, wood frame structure with a steeple and bell tower. Wright graduated from eighth grade here in 1909 among a class of 28.

In the summer of 1909, a hurricane devastated Rock Island. Jacob covered the windows of their house with table boards, feather beds and bedspreads, and the boys put the cows in the shed.

Finally the wind died down, the sun came out, and they thought the storm was over. However, another cloud appeared from the opposite direction. Gertie and her husband, Frank Wagar, recalled the storm, which lasted three or four days: "The wind came up and we got it from another direction. My dad told the boys to get the cows out of the barn real quick because he was afraid they'd get penned in. They got the cows out, and it (the storm) took the barn down."

Frank was at work at the soda fountain in the drug store when the storm came. He said they "braced the north side of the building with 2 x 6's from the lumberyard." He said the storm "racked them some" when it first came from the south. "Then about evening, it laid down for a little bit. The sun came out, and we thought it was over. People started home from their stores. I got home, but some of them had to stay in ditches to keep things from hitting them, and they never got home until morning because after the wind turned, it was worse than when it came from the south. It took down our bank building which was made of cement blocks. It took down the building where I worked and the hardware store, then another one or two, and it moved quite a few houses off their foundations."

The Wagars, who had moved with the Smalls from Illinois to Texas, relocated to Nash, Oklahoma, after the storm. In 1911, Jacob also moved his family to Nash. The train ride from Rock Island to north central Oklahoma was more than a thousand miles. Wright rode in a boxcar with the farm animals and the most valuable family belongings.

STARTING OVER IN OKLAHOMA

Characteristic of the times, Jacob was a "horse trader." He was good and usually came out ahead. In 1897, he traded Illinois land for the Texas farm. In 1911, after the hurricane took most of Rock Island, Jacob traded the Texas farm for a farm and mercantile store in Nash, Oklahoma. Jacob managed the farm in Oklahoma, and the two oldest boys, Emery, 23, and Wright, 21, operated the store. Jacob raised cattle and grew strawberries for market. Meanwhile, nine-year-old Elmer ran the family's one-horse delivery wagon, hauling eggs and chickens to the railroad depot for shipment about 30 miles to Enid, Oklahoma.

The mercantile store was large for a small town; it was also the only mercantile store in Nash. One side was stocked with dry goods and clothing; the other, with groceries and hardware. Emery bought clothing at the wholesale market in Kansas City, and it was delivered to Nash by train. Most other merchandise was brought by railroad from Enid. One of Emery's sons, Adrin, later explained the men's system for selling clothing: Emery bought it at half the retail price, never more, and sold a fourth of it for retail price, a fourth marked 25% off, and a fourth marked 50% off. By selling three-quarters of the clothes at discount prices, Emery and Wright recouped their investment. The clothing sold at full price brought pure profit to the family.

The boys ran the store on a tight budget, sometimes not able to pay bills. A relative who worked at the store

The way in which the Small family ran its busy mercantile store in Nash incorporated some of the creative business practices W. J. Small would later use to build an alfalfa empire.

recalled that more than once, Wright slipped out the back door to avoid bill collectors. These were the years just before World War I, a time of depression for nearly everyone, especially farmers. The store burned in 1914, the first of many fires that Wright would experience in his life. It was not known what caused the fire.

The fire heated peanuts that were stocked in large barrels, causing peanut oil to run out of the barrels and down

The town of Nash, Oklahoma was originally called Nashville.

the street. Many people gathered this small stream of oil right off the street to use at home for cooking – an indication of how poor they were.

The Smalls had followed their longtime friends, Rose and Will Wagar, to Oklahoma. The next year, Wright and Gertrude Small married two of the Wagars, Hazel and Frank; the brother and the sister of one family married the sister and brother of the other. Wright and Hazel were married in Oklahoma on March 23, 1912. Wright was 22 and Hazel was 18. They had two children in Nash; Earl, born September 6, 1913, and Gwendolyn, September 4, 1915. Earl and Gwendolyn were born at home.

SETTLING IN KANSAS

The Smalls worked hard to survive in Oklahoma. It was a depressed time for farmers, and even with the store, they were struggling. After the store burned, they talked about relocating where farmland looked better and opportunities came easier.

In 1916, five years after moving to Oklahoma from Texas, the Wagars and Smalls, now encompassing four family units, moved again, this time to Kansas. Jacob and his oldest sons, Emery, 28 and Wright, 26, purchased two farms in Neodesha which they operated as a partnership, sharing work animals and equipment. At that time, they still farmed with teams of horses.

Neodesha was a small community situated on two rivers, the Fall and the

Verdigris, and beside the Missouri Pacific and Frisco Railroads. The surrounding farmland was rich and black, and the town was commercially successful. Neodesha was partially supported by Standard Oil Company's first successful oil well west of the Mississippi River, Norman No. 1, which was thriving on the War, higher prices, automobiles and new roads. Although the United States didn't enter World War I until 1917, farm prices were also up as war-torn Europe demanded more food from America.

Most of the Smalls made Neodesha their permanent home. Emery and his wife, Addie, lived with Jacob and Lou Ella and three younger children on one of the two Kansas farms. They raised wheat and cattle.

Wright, Hazel and their two children lived on the other of the Neodesha properties, the Whitlock farm. Wright owned horses and cows. He sold prairie grass that grew naturally on the land, and 10 to 20 acres of alfalfa, the new foraging crop that had migrated east from California.

After four years, Jacob, Emery and Wright reorganized their partnership in the two farms. Jacob and Lou Ella moved to a farm known locally as the Mat Hudson farm. Emery kept one of the two family farms, and Wright moved with Hazel and their two children into town. The children were four and seven. Wright and Hazel bought a three-bedroom bungalow for $4,000 where they lived for another four years.

Jacob's health began to fail after he and Lou Ella moved to the second Neodesha farm. Jacob suffered for several months from symptoms of what we know today as Alzheimer's disease. Finally, he could not remember what he was doing or where he was. Wright and Emery took their father 300 miles

This three-bedroom bungalow was W. J. and Hazel Small's original residence in Neodesha.

to a Kansas City hospital for treatment. Jacob didn't recover and passed away in Kansas City in January of 1922.

Wright and his older brother, Emery, settled Jacob's estate. Jacob had deeded the farm to his five oldest children. He left half his estate for the children to divide and the other half to his wife, Lou Ella. The two boys had a farm sale to dispose of Jacob's farm equipment and livestock, and they helped their mother, Lou Ella, move to town.

POPULATION OF THE UNITED STATES WAS 106,021,537 (AN INCREASE OF 15% FROM 1910). • 1920 OF GAINFULLY EMPLOYED PERSONS,

Wright's First Hay Companies

Chapter 2

Wright Small managed a successful hay business in the early 1920s. He grew prairie hay and alfalfa, and with the help of his young brother Elmer, who was still in school, sold it to nearby farmers.

THE "HAY MAN"

In time, Wright and Elmer worked for a Kansas City broker, buying and shipping hay to Kansas City or other locations. Wright bought the hay and had it baled by a former Neodesha neighbor, John Clifton, Sr., who owned a stationary baler near a railroad station in nearby Buxton, Kansas. Elmer remembered loading the loose hay with a pitchfork. He and Wright took truckloads of sun-dried hay to Buxton, had it baled, loaded the bales into trucks and took them to the railroad station where they loaded the hay onto boxcars. Wright operated under two company names; W. J. Small, Shipper of Prairie Hay & Alfalfa, and W. J. Small, Dealer in Prairie Hay & Alfalfa. For business purposes, he thereafter went by the initials, "W. J."

Knowing he wasn't getting his fair share of the money, Wright quit working for the broker. He traveled to visit some of the broker's customers, learned their needs and sold to them directly. He began selling locally, and as demand ran out in the immediate area, he shipped hay by railroad to a company in Mississippi that operated a chain of retail feed stores. W. J. and Elmer bought prairie hay and alfalfa loose, baled, by the field or by the barn load – any way they could – and shipped it direct. In season, they stored all the hay for which they could find storage and sold it in winter months when it was scarce and they could charge

The Small brothers bought sun-dried prairie hay and alfalfa loose, by the field, baled, by the barn load – any way they could.

and receive more money. Townspeople referred to W. J. as the "hay man."

W. J. had entertained thoughts of a more formal business career when he enrolled in Draughn's Business College in Houston, Texas, after graduating from Rock Island's public school. In 1924, along with operating his hay business, he became involved with Neodesha's Union State Bank as a major stockholder and director. In 1928, W. J. merged his two hay businesses into one, to operate as W. J. Small, Dealer in Hay & Alfalfa, and continued as both hay dealer and banker.

Banking Years
1920 - 1938

Chapter 3

Although W. J. Small was known locally as the "hay man," he was a leader in the Neodesha, Kansas, banking industry from the early 1920s through 1938, the most chaotic period in the nation's financial history. W. J. had completed courses in bookkeeping, banking and commercial law at Draughn's Business College in Houston, Texas, his only formal education. Then he managed his father's mercantile store in Oklahoma. Soon after his family moved to Kansas, he began a banking career.

W. J. ran a profitable hay business on the side. Combining his savings and some inherited money, he bought the controlling interest in Neodesha's Union State Bank in 1924.

In 1925, W. J. was elected to Union State's Board of Directors. W. J. was reelected to the board in 1926, and in 1927, he helped reorganize Union State to become chartered as a federally insured national bank. It was renamed Union National Bank. W. J. was elected president and chairman of the Board of Directors in 1927 and again in 1929.

BANKING IN THE 1920s

The 1920s were difficult years for Neodesha's banks. While most of the nation – especially large cities on the East and West coasts – enjoyed a prosperous boom time known as "The Roaring Twenties," farm communities such as Neodesha were left behind. The war years had been good for farmers, but demand for agricultural products plummeted when the Great War (World War I) ended. The United States Government no longer had to feed troops, and production on European farms returned to normal, cutting back their need for American farm products. Overall, American farmers' share of the national income shrank by nearly half, driving many thousands to bankruptcy. Farmers from the Great Plains to the Mississippi Valley were additionally burdened with decreasing yield per acre from overgrazing, flooding and drought. As farm prices and land values continued to go down, Neodesha's banks suffered.

In April of 1929, the major stockholder of Union National Bank, W. J. Small, bought the holdings of First National Bank's major stockholder, Harry H. Woodring. This created a merger of the two banks, with W. J. holding majority stock. After purchasing Woodring's stock in First National, W. J. also purchased the remainder stock and assets of Union National Bank, creating one bank, First National Bank.

The bottom began falling out of the rest of the nation's economy in the

SMALL BUYS MAJORITY FIRST NATIONAL STOCK

UNION NATIONAL BANK HEAD GETS WOODRING HOLDINGS

Deal Presages Merger Of Two Local Banks; Would Relieve Overbanked Condition Here

late 1920s. In 1929, First National was forced to issue its own National Bank Notes. By terms of the National Banking Act of 1863, the government granted charters to banks, allowing them to issue notes valued at up to 90% of the par value of United States Government bonds that the banks had previously deposited with the government as security for the notes. The First National notes were ten-dollar and twenty-dollar

NATIONAL BANK NOTES

National Bank Notes, although issued by individual banks, are conventional United States paper money, fully negotiable, produced by the Bureau of Engraving and Printing under the same conditions as regular Treasury issues.

The basic designs of National Bank Notes were the same for all banks, the only differences being the bank names, charter numbers, bank signatures and coat of arms of the state in which the bank was located. Other signatures on the notes signed by W. J. Small were: E. L. Chapman, Bank Cashier; E. E. Jones, Registrar of the Treasury; and N. O. Woods, United States Treasurer. The National Bank Notes issued after 1929 are Series 1929. The signatures of Jones, Registrar of the Treasury, and Woods, Treasurer of the United States, are made with brown seals. In addition, the notes bear two signatures of the issuing National Bank, those of its president and cashier.

National Bank notes, issued by Neodesha National Bank during the Great Depression, looked like ordinary U.S. currency – except for the stamp and signature of W. J. Small.

HARRY H. WOODRING

After retiring from First National Bank in 1929, Harry H. Woodring served as governor of Kansas from 1931-1933. He was appointed Assistant Secretary of War under Franklin D. Roosevelt in 1936 and filled the position as Secretary of War in 1939 when his predecessor died in office. Woodring didn't agree with Roosevelt's policy on the United States' involvement in the war and was replaced after having served only half his term. Harry H. Woodring had been associated with Neodesha's First National Bank for seven years, owned the majority of First National's stock and was vice president and general manager of the bank when he sold his interests to W. J. Small.

BANKS TO BE CONSOLIDATED

Stockholders of Neodesha National Bank Purchase Control of First National Bank

E. A. Warren To Head New Institution; W. J. Small To Devote Time To Growing Private Business; Three Members Of First National Board Join The Neodesha National Bank Directorate

Jan 21-1938

Announcement of importance to every citizen of this community was made today when it was made public that the stockholders of the Neodesha National Bank had purchased the controlling stock of the First National Bank. This will result, in the immediate future, in the merger if these two financial institutions, thus consolidating all Neodesha banking interests into one large institution, to continue serving this community with the same excellent type of financial service as has been rendered by the seperate units. Providing as fine a financial background as any community could ask, and which it is felt by the members of the board's directors, will do much toward the continued welfare of the city and surrounding territory.

W. J. Small, president, and large stockholder of the First National bank, is retiring from the banking business in order to devote all of his time to his private business interests, which have grown to such proportions that they demand all of his time; and, in order to allow this, the merger of the two banks was arranged.

In making public the announcement of the consolidation, it was also stated that when the merger of these two financial institutions is completed, the charter and capital structure of the First National, as well as its more commodious building, will be used for the consolidated institution.

Article in The Neodesha Register announcing the merger of the town's two banks.

National Bank Notes signed by W. J. as president of First National Bank of Neodesha. These notes look like today's paper currency. They are now obsolete, but so many were issued that they still turn up in circulation and are accepted, if only by mistake, as today's money.

BANKING IN THE 1930s

On November 29, 1929, the stock market collapsed, marking the beginning of the nation's most severe and prolonged depression in history, the Great Depression of the 1930s. The downturn spiraled through commercial and industrial sectors of the economy. Consumers curtailed discretionary spending, and retailers, burdened with high inventories, slashed prices and cut factory orders. Factories consequently cut production, diminishing payrolls and purchases of raw materials, and capital goods, wages and prices fell, each undermining the other.

Money borrowed for homes or businesses could not easily be repaid when prices and wages fell, and the problems of debtors became problems for bankers. Borrowers could not make payments, and foreclosure was not an attractive option for banks at a time when collateral values were severely depressed. Banks were further pressured when depositors withdrew funds, and the returns from their stock-and-bond-laden portfolios eroded. Banks across the nation went under. Neodesha's First National Bank held on through the beginning years of the Great Depression, although not without problems.

AGRICULTURAL EXPORTS WERE $1.94 BILLION PER YEAR OR 42% OF TOTAL EXPORTS. • 1926 THE FIRST COMPOUND FERTILIZERS WITH

On November 8, 1932, Franklin Delano Roosevelt was elected President of the United States. During the four months until his inauguration the following March, the depression grew worse by the day. Across the land, factories lay idle and farmers burned crops they could not sell. As much as a third of the nation's work force was unemployed.

Uneasy about the country's economic future, bank depositors stood in long lines, waiting to withdraw their savings. Many institutions did not have enough cash on hand to meet the massive demand for withdrawals. Thousands of banks failed, taking the savings of small depositors with them. Other banks shut temporarily to avoid financial collapse. In some cities, "scrip" was used as a substitution for money.

Scrip was issued in Neodesha in 1933 by the Chamber of Commerce in denominations of five, ten, twenty-five and fifty cents, and one and five dollars. A list of businesses, pre-approved to receive scrip in return for written checks or warrants, was published in the local newspaper. Individuals or businesses not pre-approved by the Chamber of Commerce had to apply and return later, if approved, to receive their scrip. The newspaper warned against "the promiscuous acceptance of checks with the idea that they may at once be converted into scrip, as the committee might refuse to approve them." In March of 1933, Roosevelt addressed the nation in the first of his "fireside chats." Beginning with "My friends," the president explained the government's newest moves, assuring people it was safe to return their money to the banks that would open the next day. "You must have faith; you must not be stampeded by rumors..." And people did, in fact, deposit their money, returning $600 million in hoarded currency by the end of the week, and nearly $1 billion by the end of the month. Neodesha's newspaper announced that as soon as the national government settled the present financial difficulties and money began to flow through regular trade channels, the local scrip would be called for redemption by the Chamber of Commerce.

RETIRING FROM BANKING

W. J. Small served as president of First National Bank and owned the majority of its stock for nine years. He finalized decisions for the bank, while at the same time, became more and more involved with a new agriculture business – the dehydration of farm crops. His specialty would become alfalfa, a crop he had first farmed after moving to Neodesha. In 1938, W. J. retired from banking to devote his full time to the dehydrating business.

21, CHARLES LINDBERGH BECAME FAMOUS FOR THE FIRST SOLO TRANSATLANTIC FLIGHT FROM NEW YORK TO PARIS IN HIS PLANE, THE

Dehydrating Alfalfa
1930 - 1940

Chapter 4

In 1930, taking advantage of depressed land prices in the South, W. J. Small bought a 3,000-acre cotton plantation in Mississippi. W. J.'s hay and alfalfa business was operating in Kansas and he had just merged two of Neodesha's banks. But while visiting Mississippi, W. J. came upon an idea that inspired his most successful career, and which he developed into what became an important contribution to United States agriculture.

W. J.'s FIRST DEHYDRATOR

W. J. had gone to Mississippi to supervise the operation of his plantation. While returning to Kansas by train, a large steel drum on a farm next to the tracks caught his attention. As recounted by his nephew Adrin, W. J. got off the train at the next stop and hired a taxi to take him back to investigate. W. J. learned from its owner, Julius Heil, the future Governor of Wisconsin, that the drum contraption was an invention for drying hay. The operation didn't work entirely, but W. J. liked the idea. Heil told W. J. he didn't have time to spend developing the mechanics, and he asked if W. J. would help. The dryer worked up to a point, but eventually, it burnt the dried hay. Mr. Heil provided W. J. with an engineer and arranged to ship the dehydrator to Neodesha where W. J. could work out the bugs.

Early in 1932, W. J.'s men installed a "make-shift" cooling system in Heil's dehydrator, making it possible to produce a "fair grade" of alfalfa meal. In the spring, W. J. started commercial operations with very crude equipment; still, he produced over four hundred tons of dehydrated alfalfa the first season. This meal was not satisfactory though, and the first full boxcar shipment was promptly refused and returned. There were many difficulties, but as problems were gradually solved, W. J. built and operated over 50 dehydrator plants. His dehydrated alfalfa was used throughout the United States, Canada and Europe. The rotating drum dehydrator almost instantly removed nearly all the moisture from grass and grain crops, at the same time preserving valuable vitamins and minerals lost in other methods of processing. The end product of dehydrating alfalfa was a rich concentrate of nutrients for use as a supplement in animal feed. Dehydrated alfalfa, in the form of pellets, remains a valued product today.

EARLY ATTEMPTS AT DEHYDRATING HAY

It had long been observed that farm animals grew faster and stayed healthier when they ate certain grasses or legumes, particularly alfalfa. In the early 1920s, the researching of vitamins marked a major breakthrough in determining nutritional elements necessary for healthier, stronger people and animals. From the 1920s on, feed companies, agronomists and farmers sought means to manipulate animal growth through diet by formula feeding.

Historically, grass crops and legumes were dried for easier handling and to prevent mildew and rotting in storage. The age-old method of doing this was to let hay lie in the sun three or four days after it was cut, going back to rake and turn it until it was completely dry. Sun drying is still practiced, but grass crops are usually ready for harvesting during rainy seasons – and rain interferes more often than not. Sun-cured hay isn't as nutritious as dehydrated hay and the whole process demands more time and labor. Also, it was recognized over time that sun drying and wet weather leached valuable nutrients from freshly cut green hay. Various artificial methods of drying hay were experimented with, but none worked successfully.

Attempts were made around the time of World War I to dry alfalfa on large metal trays in a brick tunnel-like oven. The dried alfalfa (determined when the crop began to smoke and burn) was pulled out of the oven, quickly spread on a concrete apron, and the flames were beat out with brooms. Most of the hay was burned.

There were other early methods of drying hay with heated air. An alfalfa dryer consisting of a furnace, blower and baffles that moved heat through a brick tunnel 200 feet long was put into commercial use by the A. B. Caple Company in Perrysburg, Ohio, in 1930. Chopped alfalfa was spread six to eight

After spying an old drum dehydrator from a passing train, W. J. Small made a deal with the inventor, worked out the bugs and soon after had dehydrators installed all over the Midwest.

THE INVENTORS

Gerald D. Arnold invented and obtained the original patents on the Arnold Dryer which Heil started to manufacture in 1930. He was involved with the first alfalfa dehydrating plant in Ohio in 1932 and negotiated the first contracts for dehydrated alfalfa meal that year.

Arnold utilized a mill based on the inventions of Arthur John Mason, an engineer who experimented for 10 years on a farm near Chicago to develop a process to artificially cure alfalfa. The dryer was the key to the process and was patented by Arnold in 1916. It used high temperatures to remove the moisture from newly cut alfalfa so that the high protein content of the crop was preserved. The dried alfalfa was then ground and bagged for marketing to stock feeders.

The first drum dehydration plant was built either in Louisiana or Leland, Mississippi, not long after World War I (sources differ). In the early 1920s, the original plant was moved from Louisiana or Mississippi to northeastern Kansas.

About 1930, the A. B. Caple Company of Perrysburg, Ohio, installed a commercial alfalfa dryer in Ohio. This was not a rotary dryer as we now think of them.

The W. J. Small Company has the distinction of establishing the first drum dehydrating unit west of the Mississippi in Neodesha, Kansas. A man in Pennsylvania claimed to have a unit in operation shortly before, but W. J. Small was certainly the first man west of the Mississippi to utilize a dehydrating unit – and by far the most successful.

BANK WITH NEODESHA'S FIRST NATIONAL BANK, AND WAS ELECTED PRESIDENT OF THE NEW BANK. • 1929 ON OCTOBER 24TH ("BLACK

inches deep on a bed and carried the length of the tunnel by a chain belt. When the hay arrived at the end of the tunnel, it was dry enough to be ground in a hammer mill.

Another drying system, used at about the same time as Caple's, was a big rotating drum dryer invented by Jerry Arnold of Galesville, Wisconsin. The drum was heated by jets from a furnace invented by Julius Heil. Using Arnold's patent, Heil put the system together on a Mississippi plantation. This was the dehydrator W. J. used to launch his dehydrating business. W. J. made improvements to Arnold's and Heil's dehydrator and, beginning in 1932, installed his own dehydrators all over the Midwest.

HOW THE DEHYDRATOR WORKS

Original drum dehydrator systems consisted of a huge rotating drum with four fueled jets at one end, a hammer mill for grinding the dried alfalfa and a sacker. Hay was fed through the fiery jets and rotated in the heated drum until nearly all its moisture was gone; then it was fed to a hammer mill to be pulverized and put into feed sacks.

The first rotating drum dehydrators had ten basic parts: (1) hay chopper, (2) furnace and heat jets, (3) heat regulator, (4) steel drum, (5) stack for escaping steam, (6) cooling fans, (7) hammer mill, (8) dust collector, (9) sack filler and (10) weight scale.

Long stems of alfalfa, which could grow up to 30 inches tall, were fed into the chopper to be cut into three to four-inch pieces. (This step at the dehydrator was eliminated when field choppers came into being.)

Four large jets, usually fueled by natural gas, forced flames from a furnace into the drum, heating it to 1,600 to 1,800 degrees Fahrenheit (2,000 degrees in later years). The dried hay was ground by the hammer mill, fed into bags and lifted onto a platform or conveyer that carried them to a truck or railroad car.

Properly filled and sewn, each feed sack weighed 100 pounds when packed to the stitches. The bags were finished by hand with nine to twelve stitches across the top and two tight knots, or "ears," for handles. Typical daily output for a sack sewer was about 700 sacks, or one every fifty seconds.

A newspaper reporter, after looking into a working dehydrator, colorfully described his observation: "One pauses timidly at the din before the front of this great drum revolving at 10-1/2 RPM. Here, concentrated, are the noise of the chopper, the roar of a large ten-foot fan blowing a strong blast of air into the depths of the rotor, the screech of reduction chains connecting the ten-

Often operating 24 hours per day, W. J. Small's plants quickly became centerpieces of commerce in their host communities.

FOR MOST OF THE 1930S. FARMERS AND RURAL AREAS SUFFERED AS PRICES FOR CROPS FELL BY 40-60%. • 1929 HERBERT HOOVER

HP motor to the two sturdy wheels that bear the front of the rotor and revolve its 12-ton mass, and finally the booming and flashing of four large gas jets whose 5/8-inch orifices, under 15 pounds of pressure, project natural gas into their five-inch air-mixing tubes. The white flame from the gas jets roars to the rear of the 12-foot firebox, there to be stopped by a baffle plate. The heat deflects radially to the rows of fins that agitate the chopped alfalfa. The blast deflects horizontally, and the fins impel the rapidly drying alfalfa on through the rotor."

The reporter told of looking fearfully into the dehydrator from a ladder at the "roaring, blazing inferno." He went on to write: "After the first impulse of fear passed, and one's eyes became focused, one could distinguish in the whirling picture, first, the fierce flame shooting inward. Outside this flame then could be seen a long, revolving cylindrical, closely metal-latticed framework that caught and rotated clockwise the falling, freshly chopped hay. One watched, fascinated, the few bits of alfalfa drop through the close latticework to be caught by an air blast and white flame, and hurled, arching out beyond the baffle. The hay moved swiftly forward as it rotated. At the outer edge of the round baffle began many rows of fins that radiated heat as they impelled the hay onward, evaporating the moisture from it. The still bright green, dry hay, tumbled aside into a hopper. Through this, a blast of air sucked by a fan drew the dried hay to the fan and impelled it diagonally upward through a long pipe to the top of a long, funnel-shaped dust collector that discharged it into the hopper of a large hammer mill."

GETTING IT TOGETHER

After W. J.'s first dehydrator was up and running successfully, he finished a

The sack rooms were not for the faint-hearted. Each feed sack weighed 100 pounds when packed to the stitches.

second unit in Neodesha on October 1, 1934. He then put dehydrators in other towns and states, installing plants near small communities surrounded by rich farmland. W. J. traveled to areas of interest and inspected existing alfalfa fields. If they looked promising for present or future crops, he met with local Chambers of Commerce to talk about setting up shop near their town and ask for pledges from farmers for future business. Farmers left their names and a description of alfalfa committed for the next cutting – age of planting,

acreage, etc. W. J. could then determine the feasibility of installing a single- or double-unit plant at that location. He sometimes installed a portable unit to test the area. If a location didn't work out, he had the portable plant torn down by three men and moved by rail car to a different area – where the three workers would rebuild it in the same day. Single or double units were installed on a cement pad. W. J. needed about ten acres of land for these plants, which he leased or purchased from railroad companies or individual land owners.

Initially, the company often positioned portable dehydrators in smaller alfalfa-growing areas. The company even supplied its own power when necessary.

To make money, W. J. needed enough alfalfa to keep a dehydrator running for nine months. Alfalfa from 300 acres would keep a portable unit running 24 hours a day in the April-through-October season, while alfalfa from 700 acres would keep a stationary single dehydrator drum operational. Grass crops such as rye and oats were processed in early spring and late fall if available.

Location was always the primary consideration before building dehydrator plants. Quality and production were affected by the soil, humidity and weather; and distance of transporting freshly cut alfalfa from the fields was important because gradual loss of nutrients began as soon as the alfalfa was cut. W. J. tried to work within a 10-mile radius of the alfalfa he used, and he located close to railroads for shipping purposes.

In the beginning, five tons of chopped alfalfa hay, fed into the dehydration drum and drained of four tons of water, produced one ton of dehydrated alfalfa each hour. Only five to seven percent moisture remained in the end product that was purified – having no bugs, germs or diseases. Just three minutes after the hay fell into the chopper, it was transformed into bright green meal packed in 100-pound bags for shipping. These figures improved, of course, with field choppers, larger drums and improved heating and cooling methods.

BUSINESS IN THE DEPRESSION YEARS

W. J.'s company got off the ground at the height of America's Great Depression. One-fourth of the nation's work force was unemployed by 1933. Conditions were particularly bad for farmers, now in their second decade of depression. In 1932, a bushel of wheat brought only 30 cents, down 90 percent from the almost $3 it had fetched 12 years earlier. Between a combination of general deflation and low prices, many farmers, crushed by long-term debt, were threatened by foreclosure.

Installation of new dehydrator plants near farm communities was exciting and celebrated in the 1930s. Local newspapers wrote about the coming new industry, and there were gatherings with local bands and food at the openings of plants. Most dehydrators were built near small farm communities that had little other industry and in years when the Depression had affected the whole American economy, especially that of small farmers. The dehydrators created jobs in places where people were desperate for work. Operation of each unit required a plant crew, drivers and loaders from the fields and harvester operators, numbering at least 25 men.

Some communities could produce enough alfalfa to support a double unit requiring nearly twice as many workers.

W. J.'s dehydrators saved many small midwestern farmers from the tragedy and indignity of giving up their farms. He contracted to buy alfalfa as it grew, and the company harvested, dehydrated and paid farmers for their crops all in one day. Farmers did not have to depend on good weather for harvesting and did not have to buy or rent expensive field equipment. Neither did they have to pay labor for helping harvest their crops. They were paid cash at a time when cash was demanded for trade in many stores. They didn't have to harvest, store or market their hay. Furthermore, W. J. paid substantially more per ton for alfalfa meal than the market did for sun-dried hay.

INCREASE OF 16% FROM 1920). • 1930 OF GAINFULLY EMPLOYED PERSONS, 21.5% WERE ENGAGED IN AGRICULTURE (DOWN FROM 27%

Field Operations

Chapter 5

Field operations played an important part in the business of alfalfa dehydration, if not THE most important part. This phase of the business included (1) purchasing the alfalfa, (2) harvesting the fields and (3) delivering the crop to the dehydrators for processing. W. J. and/or his workers bid on alfalfa in the field and purchased it while it still grew. They harvested alfalfa at its prime and promptly delivered it to the dehydrators. Every crop was valued differently, and there were constant changes in the machinery used for harvesting, loading and unloading.

PURCHASING THE CROP

Alfalfa was purchased by the field and paid for before it was dehydrated. The quality of alfalfa varied, even in the same field; therefore, crops were studied and graded before bids were placed.

The value of an alfalfa field was first determined by the appearance of individual plants – color, leaf size and how thick the leaves grew on the tall stems. Other important variables included the stage of a field's growth, how many times a crop had been harvested since it was planted and how many times the field had been planted in alfalfa. As a perennial, alfalfa comes back on its own for several successive seasons. However, it does have to be replanted after four or five years.

Another determination of value was how many times a crop had been harvested in the year or over a four- or five-year period. One crop was sometimes harvested as many as four or five times in one season, possibly for four to five consecutive seasons. A crop at the end of its life was not as rich

W. J. and Vaughn Wilmoth inspect alfalfa in the field. The quality of alfalfa varied, even in the same field, so each crop had to be studied and graded before the bid was placed.

with green leaves as a crop in earlier plantings. This held true for alfalfa in its fourth or fifth cutting for the year.

After dehydrating became popular, prices for dehydrated alfalfa were determined by the usual supply and demand. W. J.'s brother, Elmer, said W. J. set the prices, but this was true only in the beginning of dehydration when there wasn't much competition.

HARVESTING THE ALFALFA

Harvesting alfalfa at its peak was crucial. If possible, crops were cut as soon as they became ripe. Rainy weather often interfered with or delayed harvests, but when fields were firm enough for machinery, almost nothing stopped the job.

At about 10 inches tall, the alfalfa was ready to be cut. Its food elements, at their best, could be captured with virtually no loss. With luck, the field could be accessed, and harvesters could go to work at just the right time. The alfalfa, if allowed to mature past its prime, would slowly lose its value.

Several alfalfa fields were usually ready to cut at the same time. In season, the harvesters and dehydrators were kept running 24 hours a day. W. J.'s field operators worked in three shifts around the clock, as did those manning the dehydrators. An observer remembered thinking the strong floodlights after dark in alfalfa fields portrayed a spooky picture, standing out as a ghostly gray in the black night.

In the first years of dehydrators, harvesting was done with tractors and power mowers. These vehicles had big iron wheels and preceded the introduction of rubber tires in the 1930s. Rubber tires were a major technological breakthrough because they increased ground speed, fuel efficiency, operator comfort and made it possible to move rapidly on paved roads.

The long green hay was pitched with pitchforks onto a flatbed truck following the mower. Drivers loaded the hay they cut, never leaving more than one load on the ground. The hay

VAUGHN E. WILMOTH

Vaughn E. Wilmoth, originally from Altoona, Kansas, married Gwendolyn Small in 1940. They resided in Brunswick, Missouri, where Vaughn managed the W. J. Small Brunswick plant, erected in 1938. Wilmoth's later moved to Kansas City, Missouri, where they settled with their twin children, Cheryl and Daryl, born in 1948. Vaughn worked closely with W. J. and was training to eventually manage the company for W. J. when he suffered a severe stroke in 1950.

The harvesting machinery was designed and built in the company's own machine shops at Neodesha, Kansas.

was delivered quickly to the mill or dehydrator plant to avoid loss of valuable nutrients. During the process of harvesting and delivery, samples of the alfalfa were sent hourly, if possible, to Small's nearest laboratory to be tested for the crop's nutritional quality.

Improvements in field work were constant. Before dehydrators were used, hay was cut and spread evenly over the field to dry. Later, farmers learned to windrow, raking the hay into rows between which they could drive to pick up the hay. This meant less handling of the alfalfa, thus preserving more of its delicate leaves. A side-delivery rake was invented that dragged behind the mower, piling hay to the sides. The long green hay was still loaded manually with pitchforks – a tough job.

Loading was made easier when canvas conveyors, called loaders, began to transport hay from the ground to the truck bed. A truck driver backed up to the loader, attached it to his truck and drove the truck and loader, straddling the windrow, as another man pitched hay onto the loader. Someone still had to pitch the hay onto the conveyors, and a man on the truck had to clear hay from the back of the truck as the conveyor delivered it onto the truck bed. When hay on the truck bed was piled high, it was hauled to the dehydrator. Loading the trucks was a science; if the hay was not balanced when the truck was traveling to the dehydrator, it would slide off the truck bed, often taking with it the man riding with the hay. Losing hay off the truck meant having to stop and reload.

Around 1942, a harvester/loader was invented that conveyed hay to the truck as it was mowed without letting the hay touch the ground to be wasted or contaminated. The hay was spread manually to both the front and the rear of the truck.

W. J.'s brother, Elmer, designed a field chopper in the 1940s (pictured left). This machine picked up hay from the windrow, chopped it and delivered it into the truck driving alongside the chopper. The hay, as it was being cut, was carried in canvas containers to a canvas elevator and then up the canvas elevator to the trailer being pulled by the tractor. The field chopper was a landmark invention that eliminated the hard work of handling long green hay both in the field and at the dehydrator.

Self-feeders were developed around 1945-46. The combination tractor, field chopper and hay trailer mowed a six-foot swath of alfalfa and threw it to the back of the machine where it was chopped and blown into the hay trailer.

In 1948, a mower head was added to the field chopper. This made one

Left: These horses were towing an astonishing 16 tons of alfalfa to a local dehydrator.

Below left: Before field choppers, loads of hay had to be pitched into the chopper which was back-breaking work.

operation out of mowing, chopping and delivery into the truck. As one load was delivered, another truck could be loaded in the field. Self-propelled choppers simply combined all the equipment used in earlier operations. Later, large tires on self-propelled choppers were a bonus, allowing field operations much sooner after wet weather. Workers could get into a field one or two days sooner after rain.

In the early years of World War II, W. J. could not procure enough trucks to keep up with harvesting, so he bought old Cadillacs from used-car dealers or junkyards for pulling the truck beds. These vehicles had very large engines and

Location of the dehydrator plants was critical. They had to be within the large catchments of alfalfa-suitable farmlands to allow the masses of green alfalfa to be transported efficiently to the plant.

rationing the buying of tires. However, W. J. obtained top-priority rating with the United States Government and was granted permission to order tires. He bought tires by the railroad boxcar for equipping his field vehicles.

DELIVERY TO THE DEHYDRATOR

In the 1930s, after cutting enough hay to fill a truck bed, it was picked up and taken to the mill. Delivering hay to the dehydrators was another part of field operations. At that time, flatbed trucks with attached sideboards were used for carrying the hay. The sideboards were about twelve inches high at the front,

could do the job in a pinch. The vehicle engines were also used in blenders.

Rubber tires were sometimes hard to acquire during the war. In December 1941, after the Japanese attacked Pearl Harbor, the government instituted a ban on the sale of tires. Wartime tire quotas were issued on January 15, 1942,

and slanted to the rear of the truck to about six inches in height.

Geared, hand-crank hoists were installed underneath the trucks' flat-beds. For delivery of hay at the mill, the front of the truck bed was lifted by manually cranking the hoist, allowing the hay to slide off the back of the truck. Unloading with a hoist was considered upscale, according to dehydrator Rodger Shinn. He stated that earlier unloading was done by tying a heavy log chain around the hay, fastening the chain to a post behind the truck and driving the truck out from under the hay.

"Another method," Shinn said, "was to back up the truck at a pretty good speed and then brake hard so that the hay would slide off about four feet. This hay, out behind the truck bed, had enough weight to hold onto the loading platform so that the remainder would slide off as you drove your truck out."

Before field choppers, loads of hay were dumped on both sides of the mill chopper where "hay pitchers" pitched the green hay into the chopper. This was backbreaking work and impossible for two men to do continuously for eight hours. Three men were put on this job; each pitched hay for half an hour and then rested for 15 minutes. In later years, the long green hay was pitched onto a pit conveyer that carried it to the chopper. Rolling hay onto a conveyer was much easier.

When field choppers came along, this step at the dehydrator was eliminated.

The Mills

Chapter 6

W. J. Small's 50 alfalfa mills were spread across five states but almost always in the midst of rural communities and adjacent to railway tracks.

Alfalfa mills were the beating heart of the W. J. Small companies. In the 20 years after successfully operating his first drum dehydrator, W. J. installed over 50 dehydrator mills (or alfalfa plants) in Kansas, Oklahoma, Nebraska, Missouri and Arizona. Crops were bought in the field, harvested, brought to the mills to be processed and bagged, and either taken by truck, or shipped directly from the mill by railroad, to a warehouse distribution point. In later years, mills and warehouses were often built together.

THE MILL SITES

Mills were located in countrysides and, if possible, beside railroad access. Railroad spurs were sometimes built by the railroad off the main tracks where rail cars could load and get back on the main track. A Santa Fe Railroad stop near W. J.'s mill at Howard, Kansas, that shipped a lot of alfalfa, was named Howard Branch-Small. Some of the mills had blenders and warehouses, small and large. Mill sites changed with the times.

Besides the big drum(s), dehydrator plants included a machine shop and small office, funnels for receiving the dried alfalfa for grinding and sifting out any metal picked up in the fields and a loading dock for bagging, weighing, sewing and shipping the filled bags.

Green hay delivered to a mill was unloaded with pitch forks onto a conveyor belt and fed into the rotating knives of a chopper (this was before field choppers). The chopper knives were

THE BOONVILLE DAILY NEWS.
TUESDAY, MARCH 18, 1941.

WORK STARTED ON HUGE ALFALFA DEHYDRATION UNIT BY W. J. SMALL CO.

Plant Near Devine Elevator Is Eighth In System

IN OPERATION THIS SPRING

Firm To Do Own Harvesting of Crop In Field

The W. J. Small Company has begun construction of an alfalfa dehydration plant on a site adjacent to the Katy tracks about one-fourth miles west of the north end of the highway bridge over the Missouri River.

ALFALFA PLANT MAY COME HERE IN PERMANANCE

Sept 23, 1941

Equipment Likely to Try Outlook, Boon to Farmers

Matt Guilfolye, president of the Abilene Chamber of Commerce, announced today that Abilene may be the center of activity for the operation of an alfalfa dehydrating plant.

A committee of the Chamber of Commerce met with Mr. W. J. Small yesterday afternoon to discuss the requirements needed to put a dehydrating plant into operation. Mr. Small arrived by private plane to hold the conference with the committee.

"Headline News"
A W. J. Small alfalfa mill coming to a new, often rural, location was big news to the community in terms of individual jobs, business for local companies and the creation of a ready market for crops.

constantly sharpened in an adjoining machine shop. After the hay was cut into short lengths, it went into the rotating heated dehydrating drum. Jets firing extreme heat into the drum from one end had to be carefully watched and regulated to prevent the alfalfa from burning. The jets were powered by several tons of natural gas; some used electricity. Maintaining the source of power was another job – some mills had their own power plants.

MILL WORKERS

The early mills employed 35 to 40 men in three eight-hour shifts; the work didn't stop. In season, alfalfa mills ran 24 hours a day. One shift usually required a clerk, foreman or mill operator, plus mill workers, a shop maintenance man and tractor drivers and loaders from the field. Every mill job was important and required hard work. During the season, mills were under pressure to maintain maximum production. Glenn Hill, who worked for W. J. in the 1930s, said that besides being under the pressures of the season, W. J. kept the company growing at a fast pace. Hill worked nearly every mill job there was, as did many other Small employees. These men installed the mills, operated and maintained machinery and repaired or invented equipment in the machine shop. Most of them also experienced bagging, stitching, weighing, shipping, inspecting grading and loading the finished product.

Crop samples were sent constantly into the nearest lab to test for protein counts. Paper work from the mills was extensive and done by hand – typewriters were not yet in general use, and computers were four decades in the future. Production, employee records,

A page from a W. J. Small ledger shows the scrupulous accounting practices.

equipment and supplies had to be accounted for at each location. A set of "General Instructions – (for) Company Clerks" was kept at each mill. Paperwork was delivered to Neodesha and later to the Kansas City sales office, usually by company truck drivers.

The office instructions, noting "ACCURACY IS VERY IMPORTANT ON ALL THESE REPORTS," covered six sheets and, in short, went like this:

GENERAL INSTRUCTIONS – COMPANY CLERKS

OPERATOR'S DAILY REPORT (for local use only):

This report consists of three parts for each operator:

1. MILL REPORT: A consolidated report of all milling for each shift, showing total bags milled for each farmer, size of bags if other than 100 pounds, hours of milling, names of workmen, hours for each man, railroad car initial and number into which meal was loaded.

2. OPERATOR'S REPORT OF LOADS: Number of loads milled for each grower and number of bags for each load – information taken from TRAILER TICKETS. "Check these reports carefully."

3. TRAILER TICKETS: Reports made for each load.

DAILY PLANT REPORT (to be sent to main offices)

This report consists of two parts—STOCK AND INVENTORY RECORD and STOCK CONTROL RECORD—each made in triplicate (copies for Neodesha and Kansas City offices and a mill copy).

1. STOCK AND INVENTORY RECORD, dated for the day of milling operations, shows plant name, date, beginning inventory of all grades and sizes of meal on hand, bags milled for

HISTORY OCCURRED IN THE GREAT PLAINS AND COVERED OVER 75 PERCENT OF THE COUNTRY. • 1935 THE BOARD GAME, MONOPOLY,

the day, bags received and shipped out during the day, final inventory of all grades of meal on hand. A section is provided for reporting inventory of empty bags. Lower right-hand corner is to show accumulative milling of dehydrated alfalfa for the year. Sun-cured and cereal grass milling are shown separately.

2. STOCK CONTROL RECORD (in three sections):

Shows bags milled for each grower for the day (be sure to show bag weights if other than 100 pounds) and number of hours of milling. The second section is for details of in-bound shipments of meal. The third section is for details of out-bound shipments. Show railroad car number and initial, bags of each grade of meal in car, destination and invoice number of the shipment.

FOR EACH CAR OF MEAL SHIPPED OUT:

1. TRANSFERS OF STOCK – shipments to the W. J. Small Company plants only. BILL OF LADING (supplies furnished by the Sales Company) original and five carbon copies will be made up as the sheets are assembled on the pad. Show number of bags of each weight of meal loaded (if other than 100-pound bags). Cars should contain at least 60,000 pounds of meal.

2. RAILROAD CAR LOADING CERTIFICATE: Prepare 4 copies... Show number of bags in each tier of the car and marks of identification of the bags if available. Get this information from the CAR TALLY SHEET. Send the Car Tally Sheet to The Sales Company.

3. CAR TALLY SHEET AND SAMPLE CANS: Operators will have tacked a car tally card in the can. They will furnish you a copy of this card and a sample can of the meal in the car, giving car initial and number on both. Try to get the operators to make a composite sample of each car instead of several sample cans on one car. Label sample can, number sample beginning with #1 for the current year, remove all writing from interior of can and send the sample can to instructed destination. Three-cent postage is necessary on sample cans. Record all samples mailed so your plant manager can know the grades of meal he is milling.

4. INVOICES: Six carbon copies of invoices went to the destination of the car, Neodesha (2), Kansas City sales office (2), and one stayed at the plant. Records kept were to be mailed the same day as the sale. Those were the bill of lading, car loading certificate, invoice, car tally sheet and the crop sample can.

Instructions for buying hay went as follows:

HAY SETTLEMENTS: Using your notebook record of hay milled for each grower (which you have checked and re-checked almost daily), compute the total amount milled in tons and pay the agreed price for the hay. Use

GREEN CHECKS to make hay settlements, making two carbon copies.

Employee information was figured and recorded by hand. Mill workers, shop and maintenance men were paid 60 cents per hour with time and a half beyond 40 hours a week. Pick-up drivers and truck drivers were paid 45 cents per hour plus time and a half for overtime. Tractor drivers and loaders in the field were paid 60 cents straight time with no overtime bonus.

There were instructions for paying minor bills, the petty cash fund of $10.00, major bills, car mileage reports, gasoline records and accident reports. Medical bills and compensation were paid by the company for several years. Records of mileage and fuel were reported to the Office of Defense Transportation as the basis for future gasoline allotments.

There was a veritable mountain of paperwork, and the office girls were sticklers for accuracy.

Storage, Blenders, & Laboratories

Chapter 7

The warehouses were part of the plant complexes, often reaching 10,000 square feet.

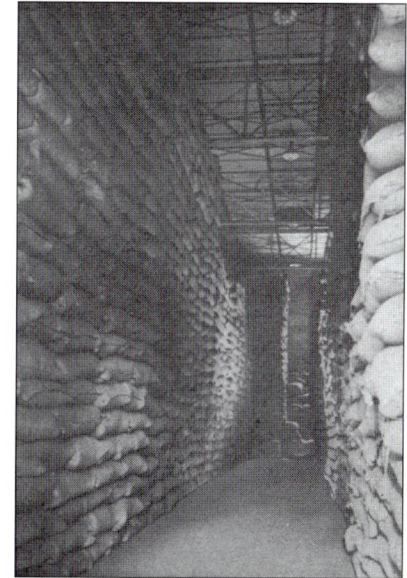

From the beginning, storage was necessary to the alfalfa business. The W. J. Small Company built warehouses in all of its business locations. These consisted of all types of storage facilities, from old red barns to huge metal storage buildings and refrigerated lockers.

In the 1920s, W. J. stored baled hay in any barn or shed he could find. He held hay through the growing seasons to sell in the winter months when it was less plentiful and brought more money. After he bought the mill in Neodesha, W. J. stored bags of ground sun-dried meal. When he got into the dehydration business in the 1930s, he had large warehouses built for both ground meal and bags of dehydrated meal. Later, W. J. stored bags of alfalfa in refrigerated warehouses; that led him to the business of frozen storage of meats and vegetables.

The Memphis warehouse was 240 feet long and stored alfalfa meal from former Southern plantations of up to 15,000 acres.

WAREHOUSES

As the business grew, so did W. J.'s need for storage. He rented, leased, bought or built storage – whatever it took. Storage warehouses were made of different materials, and W. J. built larger facilities as he needed them. During the 1920s and 1930s, warehouses were usually hollow tile or brick, or both; existing big red barns were made of wood and rock. In 1946, W. J. hired an engineer, Mike Casserly, to design new warehouses made with corrugated metal. These custom-built warehouses were designed to meet area needs; some included offices, bathing facilities and laboratories. The company had four warehouses in Neodesha, the largest of which was brick tile; it measured 80 feet by 125 feet and held 2,500 tons of bagged alfalfa meal – enough to fill 80 boxcars. The bags in this warehouse could be stacked 30 feet high.

W. J. maintained 22 warehouses in 1946. He built storage in Neodesha and Kansas City, Kansas; Brunswick, Kansas City and St. Louis, Missouri; Decatur, Illinois; and Memphis, Tennessee. The main distribution center warehouses – Kansas City, Kansas; St. Louis, Decatur, and Memphis – were located strategically for advantageous freight rates.

Rollin Vandever was a key figure at W. J.'s warehouses for nine years beginning in June 1939. He worked in Neodesha and Kansas City, Kansas; Decatur, Illinois; and Toledo, Ohio. He also managed storage and shipping in Memphis, Tennessee.

Vandever talked about his work at a couple of the warehouses. He said meal was received in labeled bags and stacked according to their Vitamin A content. Orders came to the warehouse for bags of meal containing 12%, 17% or 22% Vitamin A or for formula mixes specified for hogs, chickens, etc. To fill the contracts or orders, a crew of six men blended, weighed and re-sacked the bags of meal. They sewed the bags shut by hand and re-labeled them; a tag listing proportions of ingredients in the feed was attached to every bag shipped out of the warehouses. (Later, that information was printed directly on the feed sacks.) The bags were then loaded onto railroad boxcars for shipping. Local orders went out by truck.

In 1941, W. J. sent Rollin from the warehouse in Kansas City to open a warehouse in Toledo, Ohio. Vandever and five workers from Neodesha drove a 1937 four-door sedan from Kansas City to Ohio, pulling a two-wheeled trailer loaded with cardboard tags for labeling meal bags. He said the trailer filled with labels was heavy, that he had to take corners very carefully, or the trailer would slide across the road.

They arrived to a big empty warehouse W. J. had leased near a railroad. Alfred Wilhite, from Fredonia, Kansas, was already there to manage the warehouse. Vandever and Wilhite hired some extra help and went to work, first constructing blenders and loading docks with materials W. J. had shipped. They were to receive different grades of alfalfa meal from locations in the West, blend it with lesser grades to contain specified amounts of Vitamin A, and ship it to buyers in the East.

After a year, W. J. closed the Ohio warehouse because Toledo was too far from the best alfalfa, making freight costs too high. Other operating costs also ran high because of the distance from other company operations. According to Rollin, the company shipped out more meal than it received, finally running out of inventory. At that point, they sold the loading docks to the warehouse owner.

Vandever went back to work in Neodesha for six weeks, then to Decatur, Illinois, to set up a plant. In September 1942, he relocated to Memphis, Tennessee, where he settled for four and a half years to manage another new warehouse. The Memphis warehouse was of steel construction, 240 feet long and 80 feet wide. (A standard football field is 300 feet by 160 feet.) It was equipped with blenders and grinders and was situated beside the Missouri Pacific Railroad track.

Vandever explained that plantation owners in the South had discovered that cotton grew better if they rotated it with alfalfa. So they grew, harvested and dehydrated alfalfa. He said they had their own dehydrators but needed a market for the finished product. The plantations were big – some were 10,000 to 15,000 acres – and they produced a lot of alfalfa. W. J. bought alfalfa around Memphis and stored it until he could ship it out. He sold the dehydrated meal to huge feed cooperatives in the East.

The Memphis warehouse was an ingenious idea, but soon after W. J. opened it, the United States entered World War II. Finding enough employees, which was already a problem, suddenly became worse as men were drafted to fight in the War. Vandever found many of his employees weekly from a street corner in Memphis and brought them to the warehouse by the truckload. Some of these were good workers and some weren't.

Boxcars were hard to obtain. Rollin once bargained with an engine foreman at the switch track to trade a pint of whiskey for a boxcar. Rollin left to buy the whiskey, and there was a boxcar waiting for him when he returned. The foreman had stolen the car for Rollin, and Rollin left the pint of whiskey on the track for him.

In Memphis, Rollin used his home for an office. Eventually, W. J. utilized his top-priority status with the United States Government to receive permission to build an office. He erected two brick buildings – an office and a laboratory. Rollin, however, didn't have time from work to move into the office, and these buildings were never used by the company.

Most people couldn't get a car

between 1941 and 1946, but Vandever said W. J. could obtain nearly anything he wanted; in this case, a 1941 sedan for Rollin. It was fully loaded with a heater, defroster, and radio. Rollin drove to the plantations two days a week to buy alfalfa meal. He covered plantations north of Memphis in one day and those to the south in one day.

BLENDERS

The largest warehouses were also blending plants. Since the quality of harvested alfalfa varied from cutting to cutting, and from field to field, blending became a necessary adjunct of the dehydrator's operation. Alfalfa arrived at W. J.'s warehouses from different parts of the country in various grades, according to weather, soil, and processing. Arizona and Colorado alfalfa had the most Vitamin A; lower grades of alfalfa came from less suitable soils or climates. The different grades of alfalfa were blended to meet contract specifications,

to follow state regulations and to meet W. J. Small Company's guarantee of quoted amounts of Vitamin A.

Feed companies and dealers ordered meal with a balance of protein, vitamins and minerals that would enable farm animals to produce the greatest amount of meat, milk and wool per pound of feed. An order for a ton of Vitamin A meal might specify three bags of 17% protein, seven bags of 10% protein and ten bags of 5% protein. Bags of meal were selected from different lots in the warehouse and specifically blended for the customer. The bags were then poured into the blender and thoroughly mixed. The largest blenders mixed one ton, or twenty bags, of meal at a time.

By 1946, W. J. had nine major blending plants. The blenders were made at the machine shop in Neodesha and shipped in pieces to be assembled on location.

In the 1940s, most of W. J.'s blended meal was shipped to jobbers in New

York. It was sent out by boxcar loads – one boxcar carried 60,000 pounds, or 600 hundred-pound bags of meal.

Figuring freight across several state lines was complicated, and shipping expenses were high. W. J.'s shipping agent, George Harbin, monitored government regulations and freight charges from Neodesha.

LABORATORY CONTROL

Since the quality of alfalfa varied from field to field, and sometimes changed within the same field over its growth period, grades of meal coming from different mills were anybody's guess unless laboratory-tested. Alfalfa proceeded through the company's laboratories in different forms and stages; the laboratories provided immediate data on the alfalfa contents of Vitamin A, protein, fiber, fat and color. As more vitamins and minerals were discovered, testing of alfalfa was broken into more nutritional measures.

A laboratory official checks an alfalfa sample in the Kansas City plant in the early 1940s. This process was critical to support the W. J. Small guarantee of vitamin content in alfalfa meal.

Alfalfa was tested before and after it was harvested and processed into any form of meal. It was tested again several times during processing, and finally, just before it was sold. Before the meal ever reached storage and blending warehouses, samples of alfalfa were sent to the lab in small containers by train or truck to be graded between every process. A final test was run on blended meal before it was turned over to the buyer to establish with certainty that the blend conformed to contract specifications. Finally, the 100-pound bags were supplied with analysis tags for the buyer in compliance with feed laws of individual states.

W. J. maintained laboratories central to dehydrator plants and warehouses. The first was established in Neodesha in 1933. By the end of 1937, the company shipped through commercial channels to over 20 states, maintaining strategically placed laboratories at Neodesha and Lawrence, Kansas; Kansas City,

Missouri; and Decatur, Illinois. In 1940, it was reported that over one million 100-pound bags of dehydrated hay passed annually through Small's laboratories, each tested for uniform quality and content. Eventually, control laboratories were maintained at all blending plants and at many production centers.

COLD STORAGE

By 1940, W. J. knew that alfalfa retained its vitamin content in cold storage. He saw this in winter alfalfa in Colorado. Hay that stayed cold in the middle of big haystacks retained its green color, indicating preserved vitamin A. This was further confirmed in his laboratories.

W. J. described entering the cold storage market in a speech at the American Dehydrator's Association meeting in 1945:

"Through studies developed by our Neodesha laboratory, we learned that while we were able to save the

Vitamin A through the dehydrating process, this valuable factor was soon dissipated during storage. It was also determined that by placing the meal in cold storage at 15 degrees, Vitamin A could be maintained indefinitely. Now dehydrated alfalfa meal is only produced six months of the growing season. Yet our customers, the mixed-feed manufacturers, have a 12-month source of supply and with guaranteed Vitamin A as well."

In June 1942, W. J. bought National Ice Service Company of Arkansas City, Kansas, for cold storage of alfalfa. This plant supplied ice for Arkansas City and served as an icing station for Santa Fe Railways' refrigerated box cars. Two years later, W. J. purchased the refrigeration properties of Louisiana Ice Company in Monroe, eventually merging the two companies. Barring government

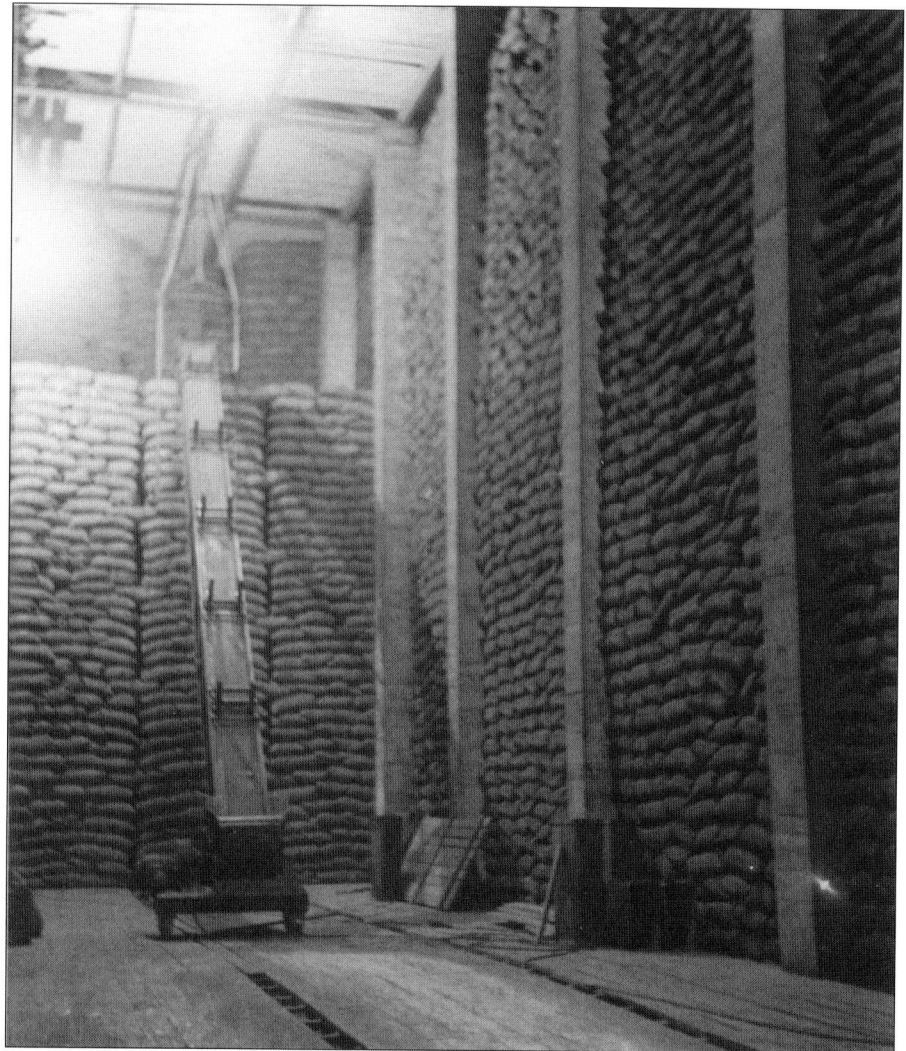

A cold storage plant in Arkansas City.

war restrictions, W. J. aggressively leased, bought and converted cold storage for alfalfa, rebuilding some warehouses to also make ice and to freeze food.

In a few short years, W. J. operated eight cold storage plants with capacity for storing 30,000 tons of alfalfa at zero degrees Fahrenheit, the temperature necessary for guaranteeing 100,000 units of Vitamin A in every bag. These plants were located at Chanute and Arkansas City, Kansas; Moberly and St. Louis, Missouri; Decatur, Illinois; and Memphis, Tennessee. Sacks of meal at the storage plants were often stacked 40 feet high. As orders came in, the bags were constantly removed and new bags stacked to replace them.

The guarantee of Vitamin A was important because the W. J. Small Company was the only one among competing large grain companies that promised fixed percentages of Vitamin A in their meal.

LATER STORAGE METHODS

In the 1950s, alfalfa was stored in the form of pellets in huge grain elevators injected with inert gas. Using gas to preserve the Vitamin A in alfalfa was more effective and economical than refrigeration. Bulk handling of pellets was also easier and less costly.

Another advantage of pelleting was that meal for pellets did not have to be ground so fine. That, together with moistening in the pelleter, diminished the fire hazard.

Pellets were a better form of feed for cattle. They could be re-ground into meal and combined into formula feeds or just made smaller for smaller animals.

The Home Office, W. J. Small, & his Employees

Chapter 8

The modest W. J. Small Company home office in Neodesha. The office buildings are still there today.

After installing his first dehydrators in Neodesha, W. J. Small installed dehydrators in 1936 at Shawnee, Oklahoma, and Kansas City, Kansas. After that, the company grew quickly, building dehydrator plants all over the Midwest. Then W. J. distributed "dehy" through jobbers to eastern markets that distributed to other countries. In 1940,

W. J. announced that the company was producing 50,000 tons of alfalfa meal annually, more than one-fourth of all the alfalfa meal used in the United States. By 1950, nearly every feed company in the country used dehydrated alfalfa as an additive in their products.

W. J. built and purchased warehouses, blenders and testing laboratories, and he maintained a large machine shop where the company's field implements and dehydrator parts were customized and manufactured. In the late 1930s, he operated refrigerated warehouses for alfalfa and lockers for storing frozen meat and vegetables. At the beginning of World War II, W. J. financed an industry in Neodesha for making war materials. This was Midwest Engineering & Tool Company (METCO) which spun off Airosol, Inc., where the modern aerosol spray can was first developed. In 1950, W. J. extracted chlorophyll from dehydrated alfalfa and incorporated a company that made deodorants, tea and breath products.

ABOUT NEODESHA

In the early 1930s, when the W. J. Small Company established headquarters in Neodesha, the town's population was about 5,000. Neodesha was commercially busier than most farm communities since it was the site of one of Standard Oil's first successful wells. Still, it was a quiet community, typical of the many small towns that defined middle-American character. There was one main street with a general store, soda fountain, hardware store, banks, a post office, hotel and a firehouse. On the side streets were churches and small, wood frame two-story houses with picket fences and front-porch swings. Farmers came to town to shop on Saturdays. On Sundays, they came in for church. There were a few newer cars around, but "Tin Lizzie" Model-T's were most common. Gas was 19 cents a gallon. Townspeople had hand-cranked wall phones and party lines. There was some rural electric service, but many farms still used oil or gas for light and heat. Most kitchens had iceboxes; some had refrigerators. People got news from their radios, word of mouth and the local weekly newspaper. TV wouldn't sweep the nation for another 20 years.

People didn't travel much and didn't

Ne-o-de-sha

Neodesha is an Osage Indian word that means, "The meeting of wooded waters." Neodesha is geographically situated in the southeastern corner of Kansas where the Fall and Verdigris rivers come together.

To correctly pronounce this word, give all the vowels the long sound. Place the primary accent on the last syllable and the secondary accent on the second syllable.

---

change houses and jobs often. Most residents of Neodesha knew each other or knew about each other and their families. Over the years, nearly every Neodesha citizen was somehow involved with the W. J. Small Company or with W. J. himself. If people of Neodesha didn't work directly for the company, their businesses, stores or farms served as suppliers, or they bought feed from the company for their farm animals. W. J. also helped many of his fellow citizens personally.

W. J. and Hazel Small and their children, Earl and Gwen.

W. J. SMALL AND HIS FAMILY

At a strapping 6-feet, 4-inches, W. J. was handsome and always friendly. He was comforting to be around – pleasant, never appearing excited or worried. People liked him. He was businesslike but always with a sense of humor. His brother, Elmer, said that W. J. was never a farmer but always a businessman. He wore a suit and tie to work almost every day, even in the field, and often wore a hat. He stood out as being confident and special. A friend commented that on W. J., a crooked tie, or pants a little too long, went unnoticed, overshadowed by his posture and composure.

W. J. was a tireless worker. Having grown up on small farms in Illinois, Texas, Oklahoma and Kansas, he knew both the hard work of farming and the dogged determination necessary to stay ahead. He grew up in a family with five brothers and sisters who worked together to survive.

Brothers in business: Emery (left) and W. J.

W. J., his wife Hazel and their two children lived in Neodesha in a bungalow on Wisconsin Street for four years. In 1924, they traded houses with a pharmacist and moved three blocks away to a large two-story brick home on the southeast corner of Fourth and Osage Streets. This became their permanent address. One of Neodesha's finest homes, this large and stately house remains standing.

The Smalls lived as routinely as they could, beginning each day with a light, healthy breakfast and going to bed early each evening. Hazel was a meticulous and caring homemaker, wife and mother. She took good care of W. J., making sure he ate right and was well groomed. W. J. was just as devoted and caring of his wife – affectionate, and considerate of her needs. Hazel was also W. J.'s friend, and she was the worrier when there was something to lose sleep over. Hazel was W. J.'s right hand in the company when he needed her. W. J. respected his wife as a businesswoman and listened to her advice.

A legend in the lives of the Smalls was Molly Devlin, Hazel's loyal house-keeper of 40 years. Molly lived close by and walked to work each day.

This two-story house on Fourth Street was W. J. and Hazel's home for many years and is still there today. The basement production lines run by Hazel and Molly Devlin turned out everything from Christmas goodie bags for thousands of children, to bagged lunches for the German POWs who worked for the company during the war years.

Molly appeared frail, weighing only 90 pounds, but she was there for Hazel and W. J. in every circumstance. Hazel and Molly worked together cleaning and cooking, and they both helped with the business. The Smalls entertained often, and Molly was always there.

A nephew, Adrin Small, who worked with W. J. for many years, said W. J. was always relaxed, even when hard luck beset him. Nothing seemed to upset him. Adrin recalled that W. J. had once advised him, "Never take your troubles to bed with you." That suggestion came after Adrin had reported a large Missouri warehouse fire to W. J. who was in Neodesha at the time. W. J. calmly responded, "I'll be there in the morning." Adrin said he didn't know how the man slept that night, but he knew W. J. got the sleep he needed to tackle the next set of problems.

Education was important to W. J. His own lack of formal education plagued him for most of his life. It was primary to W. J. that his family be properly educated. He sent his children and grandchildren to school and established college savings accounts for his great grandchildren. He also encouraged and financially helped others of limited means to attend schools.

Hazel often said W. J. had "a finger in every pie." Through the company, W. J. became involved with other businesses and people throughout the United States. He operated several of his own companies and employed and helped thousands of people. Another nephew, Harold, later wondered how W. J. lived so long, and in such good health, with such a rigorous schedule. W. J. lived to be 92.

The *Neodesha Register*, published once a week, wrote about the company's successes almost weekly and recognized W. J. many times for doing good deeds for Neodesha and surrounding communities.

W. J. and Hazel were both very religious. They attended church every Sunday. W. J. read the Bible nearly every night. In later years, they helped every church in town and donated to the large affiliations of such evangelists as Billy Graham and Oral Roberts.

THE PLANT AT NEODESHA

The W. J. Small Company plant and main office was at the south end of

Hazel was W. J.'s life-long confident and advisor.

Neodesha, next to the city's Industrial Park and near the railroad tracks. Here, W. J. began leasing land from the city in the early 1920s. By the mid-1930s, the Neodesha operation consisted of four industrial buildings and two one-story office buildings. The dark red brick office buildings faced Main Street in front of the other buildings.

The W. J. Small Company home plant in Neodesha included a machine shop that served the entire nationwide operation.

One of the industrial buildings was used mainly for blender operations. The other, with two offices, was the distribution point for supplying the company's internal needs for everything from nuts and bolts to office equipment and furniture. In the 1930s, every item owned by the company went through the supplies warehouse to be labeled with a numbered metal inventory plate.

A double-unit dehydrator sat near the railroad tracks. The electrical shop, which changed several times over the years, was located near the dehydrators.

The company's large fleet of trucks was serviced and dispatched from Neodesha. When fieldwork was done, the trucks returned and were parked on the Main Street side of the plant.

In 1938, W. J. added a new building in Neodesha for a third stationary dehydrator. This building was equipped to store 500 tons of alfalfa meal.

The electrical shop was expanded. Finally, a separate building was added

Much of the machinery was made at the company's own machine shop, and labeled with metal plates.

to the plant to serve as a large, modern machine shop where dehydrators and field equipment were developed. Equipment was manufactured year-round. During the winter months, machines and equipment from all the plants were brought to the Neodesha machine shop to be overhauled and painted.

Shipping was handled for all the dehydrator plants through the Neodesha offices. Freight rules varied with different crops, states and railroad companies. The rules were sometimes confusing, and freight expense had to be dealt with carefully. W. J. learned this lesson when he was fined by the United States Government for not complying with the Elkins Freight Rate Act. He'd paid freight to ship "sun-dried alfalfa meal" when, in fact, it was "dehydrated meal." In the end, W. J. fought the government on this issue and won his case.

W. J. SMALL AND HIS EMPLOYEES

W. J. ran the company. He seemed to have a handle on every phase of the business, no matter how far away it was from him or how complicated the issue seemed. W. J. made the decisions and handled business, promotions and sales. His brother, Elmer, had a special knack for engineering and oversaw (and sometimes invented) the company's mechanical projects.

As the company grew, W. J. employed a work force of more than 1,200 field men, dehydrator operators, salespeople, chemists, architects, mechanics, legal advisors and office workers. These employees were from all walks of life.

W. J. made it a point to know the people who worked for him. He called employees by their first names and took time to visit with them, expressing a personal concern for them and their families. He had a marvelous memory for his employees, their families and

special circumstances. If help was needed, W. J. and Hazel were there for them. They sometimes paid employees' families medical bills and bought children's school clothes.

His employees would say that W. J. never gave the impression that he considered himself higher than anyone else. When employee work problems arose, W. J. found time to listen to every employee. An early employee said W. J. was at dehydrator locations for a couple of hours regularly and that if anyone had questions or wanted to discuss anything, he took time with them.

When W. J. had money, he was generous. He paid for everyone's haircut in the barbershop, bought everyone's coffee or lunch and over-tipped restaurant waitresses. Associates sometimes got a laugh out of his absentmindedness with money. More than once, he offered to buy lunch and was caught short-handed – or with no money at all. W. J. tried to fit in by having a beer

with the guys now and then. He wasn't outwardly against drinking, but he rarely drank and never smoked; he considered these activities wasteful. W. J. enjoyed socializing, but his thoughts were always on business.

Men who worked for W. J. were on expense accounts. If they needed anything for themselves or their families,

BOB BLACKWELL

Robert (Bob) Blackwell first went to work for the W. J. Small Company in May, 1946, and continues to work as a trustee for the W. J. Small estate 60 years later. He managed inventory of parts and equipment, designing a perpetual inventory plan for the main warehouse. Bob worked in the Kansas City, Kansas, office in Accounts Payable until the company was sold to Archer-Daniels-Midland in 1952. At that time, he went to Arizona with the Smalls to work as W. J.'s personal assistant.

The number of W. J. Small Co. employees grew over the years, eventually exceeding 1,200.

W. J. paid for it. W. J. also loaned employees money for their homes or cars, charging minimal or no interest and deducted payments from their paychecks. W. J. paid medical and hospital bills for his employees. In the beginning, if his employees had insurance, W. J. often told them to drop it, and he would insure them.

The company experienced several warehouse fires, and W. J.'s employees helped fight them. It was thought that probably every man working for the company had fought a fire at one time or another. The Smalls appreciated their help, sometimes running a thank-you note in the local newspaper.

In return, W. J.'s employees were loyal. Elmer Small said that W. J. was understanding and seldom fired anyone. Once, disappointed with an employee for ruining a truck, W. J. did not fire the man, saying, "You can replace the truck, but you can't replace the man."

Every man in W. J.'s family worked for the company. His son, brothers, brothers-in-law, nephews and cousins were plant managers, foremen, planners and inventors. A nephew, Bill Wagar, was his airplane pilot. Every family member was a stockholder in W. J.'s corporations. His immediate family members were corporate officers and directors, or both.

The home office from the air showing the critical rail yards that allowed so much of both product and equipment to pass through each year.

The W. J. Small Company was up and running by the beginning of the Great Depression, very hard times for most people because they couldn't get jobs. There just weren't enough jobs to go around. W. J.'s nephew, Adrin, remembered that when the company needed 25 employees for a new dehydrator operation, a hundred men lined up for the jobs. He said the plant manager just went through and hired the biggest, burliest men in the group.

Glenn Hill, an early employee for the company, said, "Everyone worked hard then, and they had nothing." Hill began working for W. J. in 1932 for 25 cents an hour. Hill said everyone in the company worked extremely long, hard hours, that they "worked like slaves" because the company was growing so fast, and there was more work than they could handle. Once, he walked to the plant, a mile from his house, and didn't return home for 10 days. His wife brought clean clothes, and he showered and shaved at work.

When asked if employees who worked so hard were under direct pressure from W. J., he said the whole W. J. Small system was under pressure because of the amount of work to be done.

Hill also spoke of expense accounts for W. J.'s workers. He said if the men needed anything for themselves or their families, W. J. paid for it. Hill said if his truck broke down beyond his ability to make repairs, W. J. would get him a new truck. Employees did all they could to make repairs before taking advantage of these benefits. "New wasn't an issue because there wasn't time; the issue was to keep producing," he recalled.

Hill noted that men on the job in the depression years were creative. If they needed something, they often invented it. Glenn told a story about a time in the field when they created a way to drill for drinking water.

The work world in wartime was different from that of the Great Depression. In the 1930s, there weren't enough jobs and too many prospective employees. In the 1940s, with 10 million Americans overseas, there were never enough workers to fill jobs. Unemployment in the United States dropped from 14.3 percent in 1937 to 1.3 percent in 1943. The W. J. Small Company was desperate for employees.

A time many local people remember is when German Prisoners of War were used to relieve employment problems for companies like W. J.'s. The prisoners were quartered at Neodesha in barracks. Guards were on duty around the clock, and the camp was enclosed with barbed wire. Very few of the Germans spoke English.

W. J.'s experience with employing the POWs was good, although some townspeople were not comfortable with the situation. The Germans' labor, by contract, was cheap, and W. J. bought lunches for those who worked for him. W. J. appreciated the POWs, took care of them and made sure they had enough to eat. He said, "Anyone who works for me will have plenty of food," and lunches were packed every day for each POW. Hazel and Elmer's wife, Kathleen, and Molly packed black lunch pails with egg salad or meat sandwiches, coffee and cookies. W. J., who was outwardly against smoking, bought cigarettes as a weekend treat and placed them in each lunch box.

In a letter, W. J. later mentioned the resentment of some local people toward the Nazi prisoners. The reason was sound: Their relatives were serving in the war against Germany. A Neodesha grocery store, for example, would not sell supplies for their lunches. Most of the people, however, remember the Germans as friendly, hard workers. W. J. and Hazel became acquainted with the POWs and wrote to them later. W. J. wrote in 1945 that his company "could not have operated without the help of foreign labor."

The POWs left Neodesha in December 1945. When they were preparing to go back to Germany, several of the prisoners tried to escape so they could remain in the United States. Their escape was unsuccessful.

A local reporter wrote about the W. J. Small Company, "Although it has grown into a larger industry, the company has retained the best qualities of a one-man organization, giving the problems, ills and sorrows of its many employees attention and helping them in every need."

OTHER BUSINESS IN NEODESHA

Besides the major business of dehydrating alfalfa and making the company's machinery in Neodesha, the W. J. Small Company operated a molasses mixing plant where bran, straw, corn and dairy rations were blended and sold. In 1937, it was reported that 800,000 gallons of imported blackstrap molasses from Cuba were blended into different kinds of stock and dairy feeds.

An independent machine shop was put into operation at Neodesha for making dehydrators and large field machinery. Most of this machinery was used by the W. J. Small Company. W. J. also sold dehydrators and other machinery to other businesses. During World War II, W. J. funded Midwest Engineering Company and Airosol, both extremely busy war production businesses described in the following chapter.

In 1950, W. J. founded American Chlorophyll Company for the extraction of chlorophyll, carotene, zanthophylls and other valuable minerals from alfalfa. The plant in Neodesha extracted the chlorophyll by grinding alfalfa extra fine, mixing it with water, pouring it over milk dryers and peeling the residue off the drums. The liquid chlorophyll was initially used in breath fresheners and body deodorants.

SUPPORTING NEODESHA

It was written in 1940 that "every item that goes into Small's dehydrated alfalfa meal manufactured at Neodesha, with the exception of the burlap bags, is produced in Neodesha territory."

W. J. made it a point to support his community. He purchased natural gas from Consolidated Gas Utilities and Union Gas Company. Electric power came from the municipal power plant in Neodesha. Gasoline to run the fleet of trucks and tractors, about 2,000 gallons per week, was purchased from the local refinery, and oil and greases came from local representatives of various oil companies. Thousands of tons of finished product were moved out of Neodesha via the Frisco and Missouri Pacific railroads, with the exception of that delivered in closer territories by company trucks or picked up at local warehouses. The freight bill ran nearly $400,000 a year.

In 1943, Standard Oil listed the lubricants needed to prepare W. J. Small Company plants for spring operation in a trade industry publication. The article began by saying, "Figures Talk. Some idea of the tremendous importance of lubricants in this vital industry is shown by the following products destined for the W. J. Small Company:

• 4,500,000 gallons Ind. "C" fuel oil
• 750,000 gallons No. 2 fuel oil
• 500,000 gallons of Standard Red and White Crown Gasolines
• 25 bbl. Polar Machine Oil
• 35 bbl. Nonpareil Diesel Oil
• 25 tons various greases"

World War II, METCO & Airosol, Inc

Chapter 9

In 1940, The W. J. Small Company shipped dehydrated alfalfa to 23 states. Seventeen dehydration drums were in operation in nine locations, cold storage plants were established at five locations in four states. The company manufactured most of its dehydrator equipment and field machinery at its machine shop in Neodesha.

However, this era of complex, feverish productivity was to be interrupted by dynamic developments abroad.

WORLD WAR II

The 1940s brought the war years and another period of drastic change for the company, as well as for the rest of the United States and world. As America pulled out of its Great Depression, powerful dictators seized advantage of depressed economies in Europe, gaining power in Germany and Italy. In Germany, Adolph Hitler ended elections and arrested anyone who opposed him. He imprisoned and exterminated Jews, intellectuals and others who opposed his Nazi policies and sent a formidable army to conquer Europe. Japan, like European dictatorships, wanted new lands and a larger empire and built up its army. Japan fought with China and pushed into Southeast Asia.

In August 1940, Hitler's planes began bombing England, and Germany and Italy formed an Axis Pact with Japan. The United States poured war goods into England and became steadily more involved through 1941.

Meanwhile, America's relations with Japan deteriorated. On the morning of December 7, 1941, Japanese planes attacked the United States naval base at Pearl Harbor, Hawaii, thrusting the United States into the thick of World War II. Congress declared war on Japan December 8; three days later, Germany and Italy responded by declaring war on the United States. Ten million Americans were drafted by the United States selective service.

America's industrial and economic system quickly converted to the needs of war. Having created the War Resources Board, President Franklin Delano Roosevelt asked Congress in May 1940 for $1 billion to modernize the military and to produce 50,000 airplanes a year. The War Production Board, under Donald M. Nelson, directed industry and allocated manufacturing materials to the most essential war production, preparing factories to build tanks, airplanes and ships. Help was urgently needed; soon, every industry in the nation became involved in military and war production.

Demand for critical metals prompted federal restrictions on the production of farm machinery. The government asked that machine shops, such as W. J.'s, convert their resources into building war materials. Facilities

and tools were needed for war effort.

At this time, two important new W. J. Small companies evolved for making war materials – Midwest Engineering and Tool Company (METCO) and Airosol. After the war, Airosol was incorporated, bought METCO, and stayed in business to produce peacetime goods. METCO/Airosol is where an important aerosol spray can was invented and patented. The Airosol company is still in business in Neodesha, more than 60 years later.

METCO

At the beginning of the war, two men whom W. J. had consulted on a diesel engine project for the Brunswick, Missouri, plant came to him for capital to start up a machine shop. One of the men remembered that W. J. was building a new shop in Neodesha, and since there was a government hold on producing farm machinery, he asked if they could take over

W. J.'s building for making war materials.

W. J. did not give up his new building, but he liked the two men, their expertise, ambition and credentials. He loaned them money to get started. Having been in the business, he knew the space requirements for a machine shop, and he set them up at another location. He leased an old one-story brick building in Neodesha for the shop. Thus began the organization of Midwest Engineering and Tool Company late in February 1942, and later, that of Airosol Corporation.

The two men were M. H. Johnson and Clifford W. Greenwood. Both were staff members of an industrial consulting and engineering firm in St. Louis and were designing a gun turret plant for the Emerson Electric Company.

The Midwest Engineering and Tool Company began as a partnership between Greenwood, Johnson, W. J. Small and his wife, Hazel Small. They called it METCO.

The brick building was the old abandoned Geiser & Bogue Machine Shop on West Main Street. Once a blacksmith shop, it had been converted into a garage for making oil field equipment. According to the newspaper, "...they hauled away 84,000 pounds of junk" to clean it up.

Production began with three old machines still intact at the shop, a few lathes and drill presses, a planer and a punch press. Clifford Greenwood started as production manager, and M. H. Johnson was engineer in charge of designs and sales. The first employees to work for METCO were John Geiser, Rex Showers, W. D. Taylor, Milt High, Zeke Briles and Bob Bacon. Bill Hunt and Archie Blevins began work in the second week as precision tool makers, and Betty Black was hired to work in the office. In another two weeks, J. T. Searle, Sherman Dillon, Fred Davis, Don Reames and Bill Logan joined the company.

Aug 2 -45 Established in 1883

NEODESHA'S NEW INDUSTRY ATTRACTING WIDE ATTENTION.

MIDWEST ENGINEERING & TOOL CO. OF NEODESHA PROFITS FROM START; APPROXIMATELY 400 NOW ON PAY ROLL; STUDY POSTWAR MANUFACTURE.

———

Prospects For the Post-War Era In Neodesha Are Exceedingly Bright.

MONDAY, MAY 11, 1942

NEWEST INDUSTRY EXPANDS RAPIDLY IN WAR PRODUCTION

New Departments Added To Company

The War Effort translated into big business for manufacturing plants that W. J. Small incubated in Neodesha.

A VIGOROUS INFANT INDUSTRY ENLIVENS SMALL KANSAS TOWN

The Midwest Engineering & Tool Co. of Neodesha, Profitable From the Start, Utilizes Old Buildings, Puts Out a Big Pay Roll and Claims Promising Future After the War Contracts End—Has a Plant in Fredonia, Too.

Greenwood and Johnson went to Wichita, where the airplane industry was booming, and came back with contracts for manufacturing precision tools and dies for airplane plants. They began the business with more demand for their products than they could fulfill.

Two months after setting up shop, METCO had an A-1 priority rating with the government and was turning a profit. The company received so many contracts from aircraft factories that 25 – 50 more men were added to the payroll, and a night shift was started. Although skilled employees were hard to obtain, METCO planned to add 120 more employees within another 60 days, a third full shift for operating around the clock.

Equipment was also in short supply. Even with a top priority rating, new and used machines were difficult for METCO to obtain to keep up with the company's fast growth.

The nation's industrial might in-creased, and many other small com-munities told the same success story. Thousands of new industrial shops, most owned by the government, dotted the productive face of America. Shops already turning out peacetime products switched to making unfamiliar war materials and were suddenly swamped with contracts. They made gun barrels, firing mechanisms, cartridge cases, periscope mounts, helmet liners and canteens – a list that covered many pages in government inventories. Factories stayed open around the clock, and workers turned out more than anyone had thought they could. It was called a "miracle of production."

On May 1, 1942, METCO opened a second branch for making airplane parts. Two weeks later, they leased another building on Fourth Street for a consulting engineer and tool design service. A fourth and final manufacturing phase was opened in July for satisfying contracts.

Contracts arrived so quickly that an abandoned "chicken factory" at Fredonia, fifteen miles from Neodesha, was converted into a subsidiary. Now 400 men and women, drawn from local farms, and the ranks of sales clerks, schoolteachers and housewives, were being paid almost a million dollars a year by METCO. They received from 60 cents an hour for beginners to $1.26 an hour. They worked six 10-hour shifts each week, with time and a half for over 40 hours and double time if they pulled a seventh successive day. The workers didn't take vacations; they were needed on the job. Instead of a vacation, they received an extra check for two weeks' pay.

Early in 1943, the Smaller War Plants Corporation (SWPC) at Kansas City assisted METCO in obtaining subcontracts from North American Aviation and Sheffield Steel Corporations in Kansas City, and with a Pratt & Whitney plant at Kansas

METCO was such a success that a second and much larger manufacturing plant was opened within a couple of years.

City. In October 1943, the SWPC leased more hard-to-get machine tools for METCO. In three years, METCO was operating three plants in Neodesha and a branch plant in Fredonia. The Neodesha plants employed about 200 persons and were hiring more employees as fast as help was available. The parent plant, located at 9th and Main Streets, made machinery, and the other three plants made all of the precision tools used in the other three plants.

AIROSOL and DDT

One of the main war products of METCO was a steel container used for shipping 105-mm shells. The original plant made the canisters, or containers, and sent them to the Fourth Street plant for finishing. A "bug bomb" was developed from these canisters, facilitated by the invention of an aerosol can at METCO to meet the need to exterminate disease-carrying flying insects. Sixteen-ounce canisters,

made at the parent plant, were filled at the plant in Fredonia with DDT. So many orders were placed for these bug bombs that a separate corporation, Airosol, was established.

About the time World War II started in 1939, the synthetic compound DDT (discovered by German chemist Orthmar Zeidler in 1874), attracted the interest of the scientific community when a Swiss chemist, Paul Muller, realized its insecticidal value. American entomologists and chemists verified its effectiveness when a sample was received from Switzerland in 1942.

In 1940, a chemist, Lyle D. Goodhue, and an entomologist, W. N. Sullivan, both of the Department of Agriculture, were searching for a way other than oil sprays to apply insecticides in the form of very fine particles. They first tried burning mixtures of derris or pyrethrum, cornstalks and sodium nitrate to produce a smoke. This was effective, but a large part of the

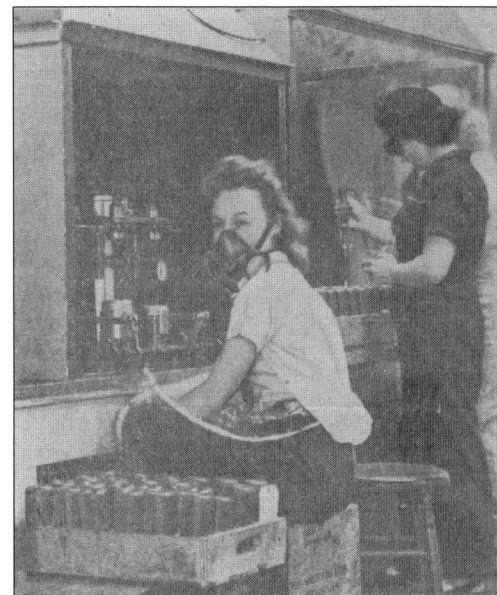

HALF OF THE 400 EMPLOYEES IN THE NEODESHA, KAS., VENTURE INTO SMALL-TOWN MANUFACTURING ARE WOMEN. IN THE TOP PICTURE, WOMEN ARE FILLING THE STEEL CYLINDERS WHICH SPRAY DDT FOR SOLDIERS IN THE PACIFIC TO KILL MOSQUITOES, FLIES AND OTHER DISEASE-SPREADING INSECTS. TYPICAL OF WOMEN WORKERS IS MRS. JEANETTE ELAM (CENTER), HOUSEWIFE AND MOTHER OF TWO CHILDREN.

Like elsewhere in the country women were a big part of the METCO and Airosol Company's labor forces during the War years.

insecticide was destroyed in the combustion process. A better method was found to be the spraying of a

FLY DDT TO POLIO AREA

Five Tons of Insecticide Flown from Here Today to Texas Stricken Zone

TRANSPORTED BY C-46

Texas Airline Plane Delivers Mercy Shipment to San Antonio from Airosol Firm at Neodesha

An air shipment of 10,000 pounds of DDT atomizers, known as "bug bombs" were flown from here early today to San Antonio, Tex., to be used in checking the spread of polio in Texas. The "bombs" were made and delivered here by Airosol, Inc., at Neodesha.

Joe Hughes, production superintendent of Airosol, delivered the insecticide here last night by truck, which after delivery at San Antonio, will be used by private citizens. This was the second shipment from Neodesha to the stricken area this week.

W. J. Small, president of Airosol, announced today that the plant at Neodesha has been making 12,000 pounds of the "bombs" daily for the past year and with another plant is expected to be opened by the company at Fredonia within the next two weeks, this amount is expected to be stepped up to between 15,000 and 20,000 pounds per day.

The plane sent here for the mercy shipment, was a C-46 owned by Slick Airlines, arriving at 6:07 a. m. and departing for San Antonio at 7:15 a. m.

Earlier this week the company shipped 12,000 DDT units to Texas by truck, as the entire production of the plant is expected to be diverted from other areas and sent to Texas to aid in combatting the spread of polio, it was explained.

Freight Airline Hauls DDT from Here to Polio Stricken Area

May 17 – 1945

Early today a C-46 twin-engine plane landed in Coffeyville on a mercy flight and flew five tons of DDT insecticide, manufactured by Airosol, Inc. at Neodesha, to San Antonio, Tex., where it will be distributed for use against the spread of polio in that area, which already has claimed several lives. Seen in the picture is the large plane and the truck which transported the DDT here. Standing in the door of the plane is Joe Hughes of Neodesha, production superintendent of Airosol, and on the truck is a CAAF fireman and the truck driver, aiding in loading the ship for a hurried flight to Texas.

Towards the end of the war, METCO was producing 12,000 pounds of DDT "bugbombs" for the Armed Services daily. Civilian applications were also developed for the product, such as checking polio outbreaks.

solution of the insecticide onto a hot plate or another heated surface.

Still not satisfied with the efficiency of the process, the scientists got the idea of dissolving the insecticide in a liquefied gas under pressure in a container and allowing the solution to escape through a nozzle with a tiny opening. In that way, they could produce a fine fog or mist that would stay suspended in the air for a long time. The first insecticide aerosols of this type consisted of a solution of pyrethrum extract and sesame oil in propellant-12 in a steel cylinder and discharged through an oil-burner nozzle.

Dr. Goodhue demonstrated the practicality of aerosol cans when he soldered a valve on a beer can at Midwest Engineering and Tool Company in Neodesha, filled it with insecticide and a nonflammable, nontoxic liquefied gas and successfully sprayed. Goodhue and W. N. Sullivan described this invention in 1941 and obtained a public-service patent. Royalty-free licenses were issued for the manufacture of insecticidal aerosols until the patent expired in 1960.

The armed services became interested in this "bug bomb" as a means for protecting their personnel from disease-carrying mosquitoes in airplanes, barracks, tents and foxholes. The United States Army used it in occupied Italy to combat lice and in the Pacific to combat malaria.

METCO, which had been making 55-mm shell containers, began also making containers for "bug bombs." In May 1945, METCO contracted to produce one-pound canisters filled with

DDT for the Quartermaster Corps of the Armed Services. In June, the first carload of canisters left Neodesha.

The canisters were stamped from flat sheet steel in two parts that pressed snugly together. Each canister, six inches long and 2-1/2 inches in diameter, was made to withstand a pressure of 2,500 pounds under actual test. The canisters, when delivered to the Fourth Street plant, were cleaned and sent down the assembly line. First, valve parts and fittings were attached and the two parts pressed together. The assembled canisters were placed in a combination gas and electric furnace and heated to 2,200 degrees which brazed the various parts firmly together. At the far end of the furnace was a reducing atmosphere compartment that cooled the canisters, enabling workers to immediately solder in a safety soft plug and pass them on to the testing tank filled with water. Each canister was tested under 200 pounds of air pressure for leaks. From the testing tank, the canisters traveled through an infrared drying compartment that had scores of infrared bulbs crowded together in a semi-circle over the top. Thoroughly dry, the canisters went through the paint vat and received a special coating of olive drab. After the paint vat, they went through another infrared drying room and then to a printer for labeling.

The completed canisters were taken to filling machines similar to those that fill soft drink cans. Loaded with a propellant and exactly one pound of DDT insecticide, they were sealed, tested again and placed in packing boxes for shipping.

Just months before, U.S. Army medics in Naples, Italy, used DDT powder to wipe out an epidemic of typhus – the first time that had happened. Now the armed services were taking all available production of the insecticide in canisters for protection of men fighting in the war.

The Airosol company was incor-porated on July 31, 1945, when Airosol purchased the properties of Midwest Engineering and Tool Company in Neodesha. METCO had made 12,000 pounds of the "bug bombs" daily for the past year.

A sales organization was set up to switch DDT to civilian use as military orders ceased. In May 1946, 10,000 DDT atomizers were flown to San Antonio, Texas, to check the spread of polio. DDT aided three chief fields: public health for control of insects that carried diseases such as malaria, typhus, and yellow fever; household comfort for control of mosquitoes, flies and fleas; agriculture for control of insects on farms and in gardens, orchards and forests. On farms, it was claimed that a steer could gain 25 more pounds a year in a DDT-sprayed field because harassing field flies had been eliminated.

In 1970, DDT was banned from public use. Other presumably safer pesticides and herbicides took its place.

The Machine Shop

Chapter 10

Constant improvements to their field implements helped the company prosper. Existing equipment was redesigned, and new machines were invented.

Machine shops were a necessity to most early farm businesses. Farmers and/or their helpers repaired the machinery they used and often invented what they needed. W. J. Small maintained a machine shop in Neodesha for his first hay businesses; the shop was expanded several times over the years.

"FROM SOUP TO NUTS"

The company made its own tools, truck beds and field implements. After installing a couple of dehydrators, the machine shop made dehydrator parts. Eventually, the shop made entire dehydrators and sold them to other dehydrating companies. Elmer Small

The machine shop was one of W. J. Small's most vital structures, building and repairing virtually all of the equipment the company utilized in over 50 plants. Pictured is John Clifton, Jr., a long time welder for the company

worked as production manager of the machine shop. Elmer had a special knack for learning how things worked; he could examine a piece of machinery and duplicate it, making changes or improvements for the company's needs. In the early 1940s, Elmer invented a field harvester that chopped alfalfa in the field, reducing the amount of hard, dirty work of loading alfalfa in long stems and eliminating choppers at the mills. An annex was added to the machine shop for building machinery, that would be sold to other equipment companies. The company's engineers and draftsmen developed plans for making the parts and machinery and ordered the materials needed for manufacturing them. Hammer mills, field machines, bag-piling machines, stem-and-leaf separators, meal coolers and conveying equipment were made in the shop.

In time, the company made nearly all of its field equipment, not only

As the W. J. Small Company grew, its central machine shop also expanded in stages.

for its own use, but for resale. Most dehydrating equipment was unique to the industry, having been developed by ingenious operators of the plants. Other up-and-coming plants were also creating parts and equipment, and they were, as Joseph Chrisman said at a dehydrator's association meeting, "as secretive as a moonshiner in the hills of Tennessee." After the American Dehydrators Association was organized, members held a series of production conferences where they learned trade secrets from each other, reducing their costs.

Unfinished dehydrators await final assembly at the machine shop.

The Company Machine Shop

The first shop was about 40 feet wide by 50 feet long, and employed five people. In 1941, W. J. expanded the shop and had it equipped for making the huge dehydrator drums. The newest shop was a metal building 400 feet by 68 feet, with fluorescent lights, lathes, presses, welding equipment of every description and an overhead track that carried a large crane for handling huge machines. Some of the drums made in Neodesha were hauled to plant sites on a large A-frame trailer also made in W. J.'s machine shop. The drums were 10 feet wide (a foot wider than today's tractor-trailer) and 23 – 30 feet long, quite a sight when traveling on narrow, rough country roads. Other drums were finished on a railroad spur track inside the shop so they could be easily rolled out for delivery to plant sites by truck or train.

The machine shop was a vital part of the business for maintaining existing machinery. Parts were made and repaired in the Neodesha shop year-round. Roy Failor, who began working for the Company in 1948, drove what employees referred to as the "pony express." He traveled to the different plants to pick up broken parts and return them to Neodesha for repair. He circled by the plants west of Neodesha in one trip and by the plants east of Neodesha

Eventually the machine shop in Neodesha made harvesting and dehydrating equipment for sale to other companies.

```
           WEEKLY SUPPLY TRUCK SCHEDULE
                                              Revised April 22, 1948
             Western Division

                          Arrive       Depart

              Neodesha                   7:00 AM
              Fredonia        7:30 AM     7:40 AM
              Augusta         9:50 AM    10:00 AM
              Douglass       10:20 AM    10:40 AM
   Monday     Belle Plaine   11:25 AM    12:25 PM    Lunch
              Sedgwick        1:55 PM     2:05 PM
              Colwich         2:35 PM     2:50 PM
              Mt. Hope        3:15 PM     3:40 PM
              Ellinwood       6:10 PM     6:25 PM
              Larned          7:20 PM                Overnight (Larned Hotel)

              Larned (Frizell)            7:30 AM
              Garden City mill 10:35 AM  10:45 AM
   Tuesday    Deerfield mill  11:00 AM   11:10 AM
              Holcomb         11:25 AM   12:30 PM    Lunch
              Gothenburg       6:30 PM               Overnight (Flatt Hotel)

              Willow Island    7:00 AM    7:10 AM
              Cozad            7:25 AM    7:45 AM
              Lexington        8:10 AM    8:20 AM
   Wednesday  Elm Creek        8:55 AM    9:05 AM
              Mentor           4:25 PM    4:50 PM
              Marion           6:35 PM               Overnight (Elgin Hotel)

              Marion                      7:15 AM
   Thursday   Eureka           9:35 AM    9:50 AM
              Neodesha        11:35 AM

        The truck will not depart from each plant until the time shown.

        Supply Orders for this trip should be in Neodesha before
        Saturday morning.
```

Roy Failor's transit route for delivering and picking up machine parts was a dizzying exercise in driving Midwestern back roads.

the next trip, almost in a figure-eight, picking up broken parts and delivering rebuilt parts. Failor drove about 100,000 miles each year. Dehydrators and field machines and equipment were built in the seven months of alfalfa harvesting. In the off-season, all equipment, large and small, was brought back to Neodesha to be overhauled and repainted. Men were called in to Neodesha from plant sites in the off-seasons to work on the machines. Johnny Clifton said 25-30 men worked in the machine shop during the growing and harvest seasons, and 65-70 men worked there during winters.

SIX ICE PLANTS FOR ALFALFA STORAGE. • 1944 IN APRIL, ALFALFA FIELDS IN SOUTHEAST KANSAS WERE DESTROYED BY FLOODS. • 1944

Obstacles

Chapter 11

It was sometimes said that everything touched by W. J. Small turned to gold. He turned some big obstacles to his advantage, but some problems he just couldn't fix. Fires and floods hurt W. J.'s business most. Finding enough help was an on-going problem, especially during the War years, and labor unions were a routine threat to W. J. after the 1930s. His dream would have been for any male relative to work along with him to carry on his legacy. However, the only likely prospect, son-in-law Vaughn Wilmoth, had a devastating stroke as he was training to someday take over the business.

FIRES

Regulating the heat for dehydrating hay was a fine science. Too much heat burned the hay, leaving some of it black and some not thoroughly dried or causing it to actually catch fire. In the beginning, dehydrator fires caused by heat controls were a daily occurrence.

A greater problem was warehouse fires. Some of these fires were started by spontaneous combustion in meal that wasn't entirely dry or by lightning, electrical wiring or sparks from traveling railroad cars that ignited the fine alfalfa dust. The cause of most fires was a mystery until it was learned that metal fragments from working field machinery sparked the blazes after turning red hot in the hammer mills. A bag of meal, packed tightly with other bags in storage, could smolder from the heat of a hot scrap of metal for nearly a week before igniting – then, fire quickly raged out of control in hundreds of bags of dry meal. Many fires were eliminated when magnets were used to catch pieces of metal before they passed into the hammers.

Fire resulted in huge losses to the company. There were warehouse fires at Neodesha, Shawnee, Decatur,

he Kansas City

KANSAS CITY, NOVEMBER 10, 1948—WEDNESDAY

A FIRE WAS STILL BURNING LAST NIGHT in the old Milwaukee railroad roundhouse at St. John and Ewing avenues, shown in this photograph of the area just north of the Sheffield Steel plant. The roundhouse, the outline of which is clearly visible, was being used by a dehydrating company to store alfalfa meal. The boxcars at the top of the picture were being loaded with meal from the building adjoining the roundhouse. Barring a shift of wind, firemen expected to prevent fire from spreading to the smaller building which contained about $70,000 worth of the meal.—(Kansas City Star aerial photograph by Sol Studna).

THURSDAY, OCTOBER 7, 1948

THE KANSAS CITY STAR.

CAMERA CATCHES A FALLING WALL as a section of the west side of one of the W. J. Small company's alfalfa meal warehouses at Neodesha, Kas., is destroyed by fire. More than 2,500 tons of sacked alfalfa meal was destroyed by the blaze, which was started by lightning at 3:45 o'clock yesterday morning. Before the blaze could be extinguished by Neodesha and Independence, Kas., firemen three smaller warehouses were destroyed. The one pictured was 125 by 80 feet. The loss was covered in part by insurance. The Small company maintains a sales office at 1200 Oak street, Kansas City—(Hefley photograph, Neodesha).

$90,000 Warehouse Fire Still Smouldering

Five Companies Were Called Out

Fire in the W. J. Small company warehouse in the 200 block East Wabash avenue that started at 4:50 a. m. Saturday destroyed the warehouse and its contents, damaged two nearby buildings and caused an estimated loss of $90,-000, according to Fire Chief Will Platt.

Three companies of firemen were still pouring water into the ruins of the warehouse last night as over 1500 tons of pulverized alfalfa, stored in bags, continued to smoulder. The fire was brought under control about an hour after it was reported to the fire fighters.

Chief Platt estimated last night that over 2,000,000 gallons of water had been used so far to put out the smouldering fire. Over 250 gallons of gasoline had been used to operate the fire apparatus

Raises City Losses

The loss skyrocketed the city's fire loss to $225,000 total for the first eight months of the year,

Above and left – The newspaper headlines screamed the same tragic news: Fire, more than the economy, was W. J. Small's biggest enemy. Damages to both the premises and the stored alfalfa meal was often in the hundreds of thousands of dollars.

Thank You ..

We want to take this opportunity to publicly thank the Neodesha and Independence Fire Departments for their diligent efforts in fighting the fire that destroyed one of our storage warehouses and threatened our entire plant last Wednesday night. The co-operation between the two departments was excellent. We also want to thank all the men of Neodesha and vicinity who were so helpful in combatting the blaze.

W. J. SMALL

A real sense of community: W. J. Small would often run newspaper ads recognizing and thanking those who helped during a crisis – even when it hadn't prevented him from suffering great losses.

Brunswick, Fredonia and Memphis. Following are newspaper accounts of the largest fires:

• September, 1940: The Decatur, Illinois, warehouse and contents were destroyed by fire. Loss to W. J.'s warehouse was estimated at $125,000. The fire was thought to be started by spontaneous combustion in a feedbag.

• October 22, 1941: W. J. Small's big hay barn burned in Fredonia. The barn was totally destroyed, along with 425 tons of baled alfalfa and prairie hay. Cause of the fire was unknown. The big barn, located just east of the Missouri Pacific railroad tracks, was filled to capacity with hay. The loss was severe.

• October 28, 1944: The Brunswick, Missouri, warehouse was destroyed by fire. One of W. J.'s largest storage facilities, this warehouse contained several thousand tons of alfalfa meal. Loss to the building and contents (only partially insured) was approximately $350,000.

• June 1945: At 9:30 one night, a gas explosion and fire completely destroyed the company's brick building and laboratory equipment on West Main Street in Neodesha. It was believed the explosion was caused by an escaping chemical or natural gas ignited by a pilot light – or an electrical wiring short. In addition to damage to laboratory equipment, many records and office supplies were destroyed. The explosion blew out the east and west walls of the building, scattering glass from the windows across the highway in front of the building.

• 1946: Fire damaged $250,000 worth of feed and destroyed the second of two Decatur warehouses. This fire at Orchard and 25th Streets originated from a short circuit in a wall light fixture, flashing sparks over fine feed dust covering the walls and setting fire to large bags of alfalfa feed.

• October 6, 1948: Lightning struck the warehouse in Neodesha on West Main. The brick tile building, 80 feet by 125 feet by 30 feet high, was destroyed along with 2,500 tons of alfalfa meal. The night watchman discovered the fire. Lightning had torn a huge hole in the roof at one end of the building where bags of meal were stacked 30 feet high.

• November 1948: Firemen fought a $300,000 fire for two days at the old Milwaukee roundhouse at St. John and Ewing Avenues in Kansas City, Kansas. Alfalfa meal, stored in two buildings, kindled the flames. About 12 workmen were brought from Small's plant at Lawrence, Kansas, to help move bags

of meal from the buildings. They used a 22-foot, gasoline-powered conveyor to carry the wet meal sacks into freight cars. It was estimated that the buildings held 20 carloads of meal. The two buildings stored approximately 5,000 tons of meal. Water for controlling the fire filled a cinder pit 10 feet deep near the roundhouse.

Also, in the 1940s (exact date unknown), the Shawnee, Oklahoma, dehydrating plant was destroyed by fire, and Small's nearby warehouse was damaged. Cause of the fire was undetermined. This plant had just been moved to a new foundation and was being rebuilt for processing wheat. W. J. carried no insurance on the plant.

Most company employees helped fight the fires. They sometimes drove from miles away or flew to fires in the company plane. A warehouse employee said that nearly every one of Small's

An explosion caused severe damage to one of the Neodesha office buildings. (Right)

employees in the 1940s helped put out fires. W. J. thanked them personally and in large newspaper notices. After Roy Failor helped with a warehouse fire, Hazel gave him three sets of clothing. Another employee, Johnny Clifton, said that after one fire, W. J. sent his wife money for dry cleaning.

BAD WEATHER

Floods in 1944 and 1951 stopped business for the company. As written in the local newspaper on April 27, 1944: "The Neodesha dehydrating plant of

This dehydrator plant was totally destroyed by a weather event – most likely a direct hit from a tornado.

Left – Another view of the home office building that was badly damaged by a laboratory explosion in June 1945. There were no injuries.

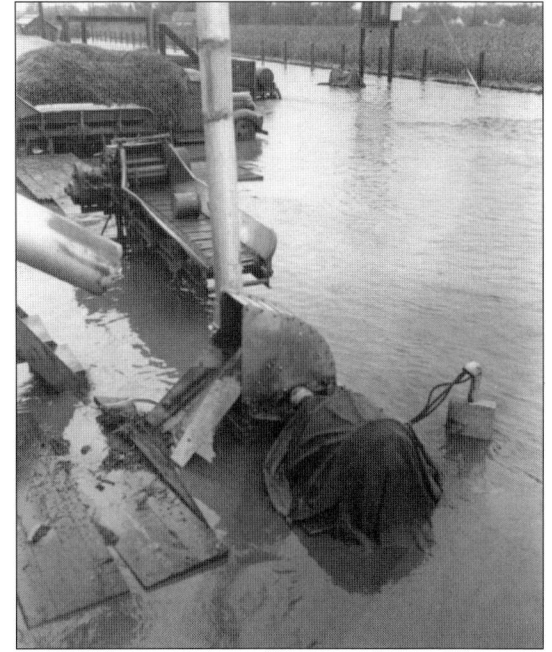

the W. J. Small Company has been at a standstill all spring, and their large fleet of trucks has been idle. No alfalfa has been received... future outlook is discouraging. Not only has the Small Company sustained big losses this season, but farmers who sell to the plant have been deprived of annual income.

Alfalfa fields on the river bottoms have been destroyed by floods, and upland alfalfa has been damaged by excessive rain. The virtual shut-down of the plant and the loss to farmers is a severe blow to the community."

July 26, 1951, W. J. estimated $300,000 in losses of merchandise,

Mother Nature could be cruel. Big floods like the ones in 1944 and 1951 could bring plants to a halt for long periods during peak production times. Not only was there damage to equipment and buildings, but the fields of alfalfa that were due to be harvested and processed in coming weeks were often wiped out.

buildings and machinery in flood waters at Kansas and Missouri locations. In Kansas City, water rose 12 to 15 feet, destroying large quantities of alfalfa meal. At Lawrence and Marion, Kansas, and Orrick, Missouri, warehouses were almost submerged. Tons of alfalfa were lost, and more than 200,000 burlap bags were under water.

EMPLOYMENT PROBLEMS IN THE WAR YEARS

At the onset of the 1940s, the W. J. Small Company was at the height of its growth, and W. J.'s greatest need was for employees. These were the World War II years when millions of Americans had gone to Europe to fight. W. J. wrote to his son, Earl, about operating the mills handicapped by the lack of labor. He didn't think the company could fulfill demand for another season.

During this period, German Prisoners of War were dispatched around the United States to ease business employment problems. W. J. requested help, and in April 1945, 150 Germans were sent from Ft. Riley, Kansas, to work for W. J. and Elk Valley Dehydrating in Independence, Kansas. They were stationed in Neodesha. W. J. often expressed that he couldn't have managed without foreign labor.

Rollin Vandever, who managed the big new warehouse in Memphis, Tennessee, talked about his employee problems there. Vandever said he was always desperate for help. He hired workers from town looking for any kind of job. He would drive into town, pick up blacks looking for jobs, and take them back to the warehouse – much like today's situation in California with migrant workers. "There would be anywhere from three to a dozen men waiting on a street corner." He said these men worked hard, but many of them didn't show up for work the day after receiving their paychecks – until they ran out of money again.

Other nearby companies poached each other's employees. Rollin took employees from a nearby rice mill, and the rice mill heisted Rollin's employees. A worker for the W. J. Small Company would inform an employee at the rice mill that W. J. was a better place to work, and the latter would change jobs. This worked both ways.

Rollin said some of his workers came from Mississippi although it was illegal to hire men across state lines. They got caught once when he sent an employee, George Phillips, to pick up a truckload of blacks from Mississippi. Authorities arrested George, took his truck, and put him in jail. Rollin called W. J. who called his attorney, LeRoy Bradfield. Bradfield said he would "make some calls;" George was released from jail and Rollin received his truck.

LABOR UNIONS

Labor unions were weak during the 1920s and early 1930s but grew during

After railroad officials re- | the site of a new warehouse for | roadway 400 feet from the | learned. Work on the building
quested them to keep off Wa- | the W. J. Small Co., near the | building site. The name of the | is barely underway.
bash property, a group of men | East Decatur yards, were forced | protesting union was not.
picketing construction work at | to do their picketing from a | | (Herald-Review Photo)

During WWII, problems on the job were seen as part of the war's hardships. By 1946, the unions were speaking out for their members and gaining strong power and influence. Although W. J. preferred to deal directly with his employees on a more personal level, the W. J. Small Company eventually acquiesced to union negotiations in Ohio, Illinois and Kansas.

the depression. Organized unions were mostly quiet during the war as problems on the job were seen as part of the war's hardships. Then, as factories turned to making domestic appliances and cars, unions spoke out again for their members. The American labor unions entered the postwar era on a wave of militant strikes, and by 1946, there were labor strikes throughout the country. Companies often used the police or hired thugs to attack the strikers and drive them off. But the unions slowly made gains in more and more companies. The W. J. Small Company eventually acquiesced to union negotiations in Ohio, Illinois and Kansas.

Johnny Clifton, Jr., of Neodesha, remembered going to a union meeting in the basement of a local hotel one evening after work. He said a "big union guy" from Kansas City spoke, and W. J.'s employees were asked to vote to join the union. Only two refused to sign up – himself and another employee. Johnny suggested to the workers that they ask W. J. for more money and vacation, but he said the men wanted to join the union for more money. W. J. later told Johnny that he wished they had come to him instead of allowing outsiders to get involved. Clifton said the union men came to town in "big ole black limousines, driven by chauffeurs," and that they talked in a tough, threatening manner. W. J. gave in, negotiating wages and vacation time. Clifton said that if

W. J. had not consented, the union would have picketed in Neodesha, closing down the home office.

A former Ohio warehouse manager, Rollin Vandever, talked about his experience with the union in 1942. He said men from the American Federation of Labor (the predecessor of today's federated AFL-CIO) stopped by the warehouse, showed identification and wanted to talk with him about joining. Rollin said these men were belligerent and played rough. He called W. J., who told him to talk along with them, reason with them, do his best. They threatened a march on the warehouse grounds that afternoon by 2,500 Toledo members if W. J. didn't sign up. W. J. again saw no choice.

A relative/employee, when asked what W. J. thought of unions, summed it up by saying that W. J. "ushered" a union man out of his office by the seat of the pants one day. He carried the man out the front door by his shirt and belt.

Growth in The '40s

Chapter 12

Eight Years of Phenomenal Expansion

On July 14, 1932, one of the first machines in the United States for the artificial dehydration of alfalfa, made its trial operation run here in Neodesha, Kansas. The man responsible for its installation, W. J. Small, a local hay dealer, never dreamed that some day he would become the world's largest producer of alfalfa meal. Today he operates, what has now become a corporation, in thirty-seven states with offices in several large cities.

[This entire article was written by a reporter of the Neodesha Register from information compiled by him.—Editor.]

W. J. SMALL

The General Office of the W. J. Small Company, Inc. Through this office passes all reports of the eighteen mills which are located in Kansas, Missouri, Oklahoma, Ohio, Illinois, and Tennessee.

The term "artificial dehydration" simply means the drying by an artificial method by the use of heat other than that given off by the sun. Heretofore, alfalfa has been cut in the field and left laying on the ground to cure. To remove the moisture by this process, fermentation takes place and breaks down the most valuable parts of the plant. By the artificial dehydration process the mois-ture of around 80% is removed in approximately 3 minutes down to 6%. Fermentation then will not take place until the product comes in contact with the moisture in an animal's stomach which is where the product should be broken down. Science has recently proven that one pound of artificially dehydrated alfalfa meal is worth nearly five of the sun cured product.

The 1940s were hectic and busy for W. J. Small. In 10 years, he had supplemented his first dehydration plant at Neodesha with 24 other producing plants, nine blending plants, 22 warehouses (some refrigerated) and five laboratories. In 1940, the company produced 50,000 tons of "dehy". At this time, W. J. was installing five new plants a year. The company had begun selling the machinery it manufactured in its machine shop which also provided the dehydrators and nearly all field equipment.

World War II led W. J. in several new directions. In January 1942, as the war heated up, W. J. funded Midwest Engineering Company (METCO) for making war materials. The war business

THE BUILDING AND MACHINERY GO UP TOGETHER.

—Ortho Photo Company Photograph.

In erecting this new building just east of the south approach to the Fairfax bridge (right), in the Fairfax district, the W. J. Small company started the installation of machinery with the building far from complete. In this way there have been fewer obstructions. This photograph was taken before the larger of the two dehydrating units, described as the largest built for this purpose, had arrived. The W. J. Small company dehydrates alfalfa and other green crops into a meal, which, because of the rapid process involved, is described as containing a high vitamin content.

Plants would go up rapidly. At this Fairfax district location, dehydrator equipment was installed at the same time the building went up.

W. J. Small Co. Opens Three New Alfalfa Dehydrating Plants

NEW PLANTS—Pictured at the top left is one of three new alfalfa dehydrating plants opened this season by the W. J. Small Co. in northern Colorado. The Windsor plant, shown in the photo, is typical of the others at Eaton and Berthoud. At the top right, Jerry Sotola, Armour & Co., Chicago, is pictured congratulating W. J. Small at the opening ceremonies held in Windsor April 15. Lower left, Francis W. Dressor, an editor of the farm publication, Western Farm Life, Denver, and H. A. Dyer, Kansas City, vice president and sales manager of the W. J. Small Co., are shown viewing some of the new equipment in the plant. At the lower right is part of the crowd of 1,500 lining up for the barbecue the opening day.

Westward Ho! Three W. J. Small plants open almost simultaneously in Colorado.

grew phenomenally and spun off another fast-growing and successful company, Airosol, for manufacturing and filling aerosol spray cans.

The dehydration and storage business continued growing along with the war businesses, METCO and Airosol. Business tripled as W. J. took on government contracts for hay and mixed feed. At the same time, the companies struggled over a severe lack of labor, materials and every kind of transportation.

HAYING IN COLORADO

During the war, there was an enormous need for food for American forces training in the United States and for allies and armed forces overseas. W. J. had large government contracts to satisfy

Insecticide Firm Buys Vacant Building to House Employees

The W. J. Small Company to Convert Property at 3125 Tracy Into Units—Former Owner's Tiff With OPA Has Kept 3-Story Structure Empty.

BECAUSE he was miffed at the OPA, Parson W. Strawbridge has refused to rent a 3-story apartment building and other property at the northeast corner of Linwood boulevard and Tracy avenue for the last two years.

The building, at 3125 Tracy, is a 27-room structure, suitable for multiple family occupancy. Parson's grievance was aired last December are being considered by company officials now, but final development will depend on rental terms and the materials situation.

It is understood one idea is to make nine 3-room units in the structure. An official of the Small company said yesterday that few structural changes will be made. A 7-car garage is located behind the apartment.

The W. J. Small company recent-

THE W. J. SMALL COMPANY WILL HOUSE PART OF ITS EMPLOYEES IN THIS 3-STORY APARTMENT BUILDING, 3125 TRACY AVENUE, VACANT MORE THAN TWO YEARS—(Kansas City Star photograph).

for training bases that were suddenly feeding thousands of men.

Already operating three milling businesses in Colorado, W. J. sent buyers to Colorado in November or December to buy all the alfalfa they could find for later harvesting, processing and shipping. This "winter hay" was "high grade," with the highest protein and Vitamin A content. Colorado hay was processed in May, sacked, and then shipped to Kansas City or another company blending plant/distribution point. Most of W. J.'s employees worked some winters in Colorado. Custom-made portable grinders, made in the machine shop in Neodesha, were backed up to the haystacks to process and bag directly from the stacks. The stacks were huge – described "as big as houses." These grinders could process two to three tons

Continued rapid growth in Neodesha necessitated that the W. J. Small Company move into the apartment business.

ALFALFA MILL PROVES BOON TO FARMERS

AT BELLE PLAINE MILL

Belle Plaine Unit, Established Three Years Ago, Works Night and Day

BUYS CROP IN FIELDS

Alfalfa meal may spell new industries for many small Kansas towns as it now is doing for Belle Plaine, Kan., where for three years a mill has operated day and night during the alfalfa season, from April to October.

This mill is one of 14 now operated by the W. J. Small company. It is their farthest west outfit and is managed by Earl Clanton.

The elements which produce alfalfa meal, in reality alfalfa ground to the fineness of dust, is the alfalfa, power, labor and heat. The alfalfa fresh from the mower is fed into a chopper where it is shredded and then thrown into the mouth of super-heaters where all the moisture is converted into steam and the dried plant blown to grinders where it is converted into the meal or powder and then blown into sacks, which are lifted to waiting freight cars and dispatched to mills. There it is mixed with grain and other feeds.

Alfalfa dehydrator plants were a financial and economic "BOON" to local communities.

of hay in an hour. Men would then sew the bags by hand, tag them and ship them by train to Kansas City.

Elmer and his wife, Kathleen, spent five or six summers in Alamosa, Colorado, during and after the war. Elmer set up shop near railroad stations for processing the alfalfa, and Kathleen trained people to handle billing and shipping. Colorado operations were managed from Neodesha. During the haying season, crews worked in 12-hour shifts around the clock. When the hay was ground and bagged at one location, they moved on to the next.

Elmer said operating so far from the home office was expensive. Costs

The Shawnee, Oklahoma dehydrator plant generated its own electricity at half the price that the company regularly paid to electricity companies in other locations.

involved trucks, grinders, feed bags, living expenses for employees, office expenses, payroll and shipping. Elmer said W. J. usually borrowed $100,000 to $200,000 to conduct business in Colorado. He was known all over the country by feeders, and the company was considered big business by the government, allowing him to borrow from banks in New York. Elmer said W. J. borrowed all the money he could, purely on speculation.

After satisfying government war contracts, W. J. continued doing a large part of his business in Colorado. There was more alfalfa in Colorado, and it was of better quality than Midwest crops because the weather was drier. Consequently, fields were irrigated, enabling farmers to control moisture in the crops. Midwestern spring rains and heavy dew often leached nutrients from hay before it could be baled or milled.

The high-grade Colorado hay was processed on site and shipped back to

Kansas, Missouri, Illinois or Tennessee to be blended with lower grade hay out of those states.

REFRIGERATING ALFALFA

In Colorado, W. J. discovered the benefits of refrigerating alfalfa. He became aware that stacked winter hay kept its rich green color inside the stack where it stayed cold. However, it lost that bright color on the outside from exposure to sunlight and warmer temperatures. Since the green color was the location of the best nutrients, it was determined that refrigeration was an answer to better storage. Through studies at the Neodesha laboratory, W. J. learned that Vitamin A had a limited life even in dehydrated alfalfa, but the important vitamin was preserved indefinitely in storage at 15 degrees Fahrenheit.

W. J. bought the properties of National Ice Service in Arkansas City, Kansas, in June 1942. In 1945, he also bought Louisiana Ice Company. These companies were in the business of making and shipping ice. W. J. converted the buildings he acquired into alfalfa blending and cold storage plants. He also upgraded cold storage properties for freezing meat and vegetables. He established cold storage warehouses at Arkansas City and Chanute, Kansas; Kansas City, Moberly and St. Louis, Missouri; and Decatur, Illinois.

By 1940, feed companies in every state were selling feed mixed with dehydrated alfalfa. Competing dehydrator businesses opened up all over the nation. The W. J. Small Company, using refrigerated storage, advertised their dehydrated alfalfa as the only product of its kind guaranteeing 100,000 units of Vitamin A in every bag.

THE AIRPLANE

Bill Wagar, W. J's. nephew by marriage, went to work for W. J. in 1945. He was 26 years old. Bill had undergone flight training and flown overseas in World War II. When Bill returned from the war, W. J. asked him if he would fly a company plane.

W. J. had not yet purchased a plane, so Bill accompanied him to Wichita to purchase one. They bought a new commercial twin engine Beechcraft with five passenger seats.

W. J. kept the plane in a hangar at Chanute, Kansas, about 20 miles from Neodesha. The plane was used almost exclusively for W. J. to travel to the dehydrator plants that, by this time, were scattered from California to Missouri and from Nebraska to Louisiana. Bill flew the plane alone, never utilizing a copilot, and W. J. was often his only passenger.

The mill managers usually weren't given forewarning that W. J. and Bill were flying in. Bill would circle a mill, the manager would hear them coming, identify the plane, and go out to the field to pick them up. Bill looked for fields that had been cut and then for landing spaces that didn't have ditches or obstacles. Sometimes they visited several plants in one day, covering the plants in two or three different states. Bill said they usually left early in the morning and returned at dusk or just after dark.

OTHER BUSINESS

W. J. established a sales company in Kansas City, Missouri, on January 1, 1941, for promoting the sale of alfalfa meal and other dehydrated farm products. The W. J. Small Sales Company operated in 39 states and Canada, handling output of the company's mills.

On August 1, 1946, it was announced that the W. J. Small Company, "one of the most rapidly growing industries in the Kansas City area," had purchased the six-floor Feld building at 12th and Oak Streets in Kansas City for use as company headquarters. W. J. remodeled three floors to be occupied by general management, laboratories, sales, accounting and purchasing departments. All these depart-

BOOMED BECAUSE OF PENT-UP DEMAND FOR CONSUMER GOODS THAT HAD BEEN RATIONED OR HAD CEASED PRODUCTION DURING

The pinnacle of hard work: W. J. Small Company sales headquarters in Kansas City (right); and the company plane in which W. J. toured his plants scattered over eight states (left).

ments were previously located in the Fairfax industrial district in Kansas City.

At the same time that W. J. bought the Feld building, he purchased the old City Ice Company plant at 18th and Muncie in Kansas City, Kansas, with plans to rebuild it and add a blending plant. The rebuilt warehouse held 6,000 tons of feed at regular temperatures and 3,000 tons of feed in refrigeration.

AMERICAN DEHYDRATORS ASSOCIATION

In 1941, the American Dehydrators Association (ADA) was organized in Ohio and granted a charter as a "not for profit" corporation. Dehydrators were springing up all over the country. Until the ADA formed, problems involving price controls, machinery, labor and transportation were settled without industry standards or trading rules. The association was born out of issues taken to Washington on an individual basis where it was learned that businesses acting as a group were much more effective. Another advantage of the association was the sharing of research, engineering of machinery and ideas for industry growth.

In January 1942, 31 dehydrators – most of the companies in the U.S. – attended the first national dehydrators meeting in St. Louis. W. J. was very active in both the American and National associations. In 1946, he was unanimously elected President of the American Dehydrators Association.

Advertising

Chapter 13

The sales division printed pamphlets and marketing materials with "modern" graphics.

The "Small's" booklet (above) has bound pages of high quality "alfalfa green" ink blotters – a 1940s style premium.

In the 1930s, W. J. Small advertised dehydrated alfalfa by talking to farmers in farm communities through their Chambers of Commerce. Feed companies advertised their feeds as being mixed with dehydrated alfalfa, and local newspapers ran large articles about this new product, introducing the new industry to small towns.

COMPETITION

By the 1940s, other dehydrating companies were springing up around the country. Faced with new competition, W. J. opened a separate sales division in Kansas City, Missouri. He advertised in farm publications for feed companies, and the sales division printed Small's own pamphlets about the advantages of dehydrated alfalfa.

IT'S A *Small* WORLD...

when it comes to DEHYDRATED ALFALFA MEAL!

Small's Dehydrated Alfalfa Meal is well and favorably known
wherever dehydrated alfalfa meal is used.

It has an earned reputation which is
the result of an enviable record of performance
in the world's most distinguished brands of formula feeds.

It is generally recognized that Small's Dehydrated
Alfalfa Meal is the brand that made
dehydrated alfalfa meal famous—
the world over

Small's
DEHYDRATED ALFALFA MEAL
FOR FEEDS WITH A FUTURE
THE W. J. SMALL COMPANY, INC.
1200 OAK STREET
KANSAS CITY, MISSOURI
SALES DIVISION

CONSTITUENTS OF DEHYDRATED ALFALFA

Research proves that no other natural feedstuff

fortifies feed with so many important nutritive factors

as a good grade of dehydrated alfalfa meal!

Top Row: Oil Solubles   Center Row: Water Solubles   Bottom Row: Amino Acids From Alfalfa Protein

Other constituents include—BORON, CALCIUM, CHLORINE, COBALT, COPPER, IRON, MAGNESIUM,
MANGANESE, MOLYBDENUM, NITROGEN, PHOSPHORUS, POTASSIUM, SODIUM, SULFUR, ZINC

Small's
DEHYDRATED ALFALFA MEAL
THE W. J. SMALL COMPANY
DIVISION
Archer-Daniels-Midland Company
1200 Oak St.   Kansas City, Mo.

W. J. Companies Sell to Archer-Daniels-Midland

Chapter 14

On August 24, 1951, it was announced in newspapers around the country that the W. J. Small Company had sold to Archer-Daniels-Midland. Located in Minneapolis, Minnesota, A-D-M was one of the largest food processing and grain storage companies in the world, a leader and innovator in agriculture. A-D-M processed soybeans, corn, wheat, cocoa and other crops.

A-D-M bought all the assets of the Small Company – "the world's largest producer of high-quality dehydrated alfalfa meal" – including the dehydrating and blending plants, warehouses, cold storage plants and facilities where the company designed and manufactured field choppers, self-feeders, dehydrators,

The Wall Street Journal *coverage of the sale of the W. J. Small Company on August 27th, 1951*

Archer-Daniels-Midland Buys W. J. Small Co., Alfalfa Meal Producer

Archer-Daniels-Midland Co. announced the purchase of the W. J. Small Co., Inc. of NEODESHA, KANS., world's largest producer of high-quality dehydrated alfalfa meal.

The Kansas firm will operate as the W. J. Small Co. Division of Archer-Daniels-Midland Co.

By buying W. J. Small, Archer-Daniels-Midland, already the largest producer of protein concentrates, becomes the leading supplier of another important ingredient for the livestock and poultry feed industry.

Dehydrated alfalfa meal is found in nearly every commercial ration for hogs, chickens and turkeys, and in many beef and dairy rations.

A.-D.-M. will take over W. J. Small's dehydrating and blending plant, warehouses, cold storage plants and shops where the firm makes its own field choppers, self feeders, dehydrators, hammer mills and other plant equipment.

W. J. Small, founder and president, will continue in active charge of all operations as an A.-D.-M. vice president.

Mr. Small opened his first dehydrating plant at Neodesha, Kans., in 1931. The firm now has more than 1,000 employes and operates 51 plants in Kansas, Nebraska, Missouri, Colorado, Illinois, Arizona, Oklahoma and Tennessee.

General offices of the firm will remain at Neodesha, and sales offices will be continued at Kansas City, Mo. No changes in personnel or operation policy are planned.

Archer-Daniels Midland Reports Net Worth Reaches Record High

Archer-Daniels Midland Co. Sunday reported increased sales and higher earnings, with the firm's net worth and working capital at an all-time high.

At the same time, T. L. Daniels, president of the company, announced the firm had acquired complete ownership of the W. J. Small Co. Inc., Neodesha, Kan., described as the world's largest producer of dehydrated alfalfa meal. Purchase price was not disclosed.

The Small firm operates 51 outlets in eight states.

Net worth of the company at the end of the fiscal year ending June 30, 1951, was placed at $85,266,750—a gain of $5,187,432 over last year and almost three times as much as a decade ago.

THE ANNUAL REPORT to stockholders also disclosed net working capital of $49,397,282—an increase of $3,517,355 since last year and more than three times its 1941 figure.

Net sales for the year were $239,868,594, compared with $219,060,069 for 1950. Net profit was $10,764,726, up 15 per cent from the $9,339,934 reported a year ago.

However, both net sales and net profit fell far short of the bonanza years of 1947 and 1948. Sales in the latter year amounted to $307,926,734 and profits in 1947 were $15,673,041.

The company distributed $4,577,294 in dividends during the year, representing 42.5 per cent of net profits. These were paid in four 70-cent quarterly dividends, as compared to four 50-cent payments in 1950. The dividend total was the largest melon in the company's history.

THE COMPANY HAS 1,634,748 shares of common stock outstanding, the result of a three-way split in 1946. It retired all its preferred stock in 1940.

In a news conference which accompanied issuance of the annual report, Daniels declined to predict whether the $2.80 annual dividend rate will be continued. He said the company prefers to issue regular dividends rather than special payments, and that future action will depend upon decisions by the board of directors.

Daniels described violent market fluctuations, caused by in-

ternational developments, as the major management problem during the year. He gave credit for the sales and earning jump to bumper crops and strong consumer demand.

GRAIN DIVISION transactions, he explained, were not included in the company's sales figure. He said grain storage operations were at capacity levels and that exports through west coast ports—especially to Japan and India—were at a record high.

The firm's total storage capacity, he said, is now at 64,313,000 bushels. New storage capacity added during the war included a 500,000 bushel annex at Tacoma, Wash., and smaller elevators at Condon and Ione, Ore.

Daniels said its principal operations were in the linseed, soybean, grain and flour milling fields.

The firm's expanded chemical research program, Daniels added, had resulted in a variety of new products. One of the most successful of these, he said, was Gypstick, used as an aid in drilling of oil wells.

DANIELS SAID that despite increasing difficulties in business operations because of government restrictions, the outlook for the next year is favorable.

Daniels said that his firm acquired sole ownership of the Small company from W. J. Small, founder and president of the latter firm, and his associates. Small will continue in active charge of the new division and has been named vice-president of Archer-Daniels-Midland, Daniels disclosed.

This report by the Minneapolis Morning Tribune *on August 27, 1951, featured photos of T. L. Daniels and W. J. Small.*

hammer mills and other farm equipment. W. J. kept the W. J. Small Company office building in Kansas City and stock in other companies owned by the W. J. Small Company and various notes and mortgages held by the company.

After transferring assets, W. J. operated the W. J. Small Company as a Division of A-D-M and served as a vice-president of A-D-M. General offices of the W. J. Small Company Division of A-D-M remained at Neodesha with sales offices in Kansas City, Missouri. W. J. retired from actively managing the plants in 1953 and retired as vice-president of A-D-M in 1955 at age 65.

The 55 manufacturing plants and warehouses of the W. J. Small Company Division employed over 1,200 workers in eight states.

LIST OF W. J. SMALL FACILITIES SOLD TO A-D-M:

ARIZONA: Mesa and Yuma.
COLORADO: Berthold, Eaton, Ordway and Windsor.
ILLINOIS: Decatur and National City.
KANSAS: Arkansas City, Augusta, Belle Plaine, Chanute, Colwich, Deerfield, Dodge City, Douglass, Eureka, Fredonia, Garden City, Larned, Lawrence, Marion, Mentor, Mount Hope, Neodesha, Sedwick and Whitman.
MISSOURI: Brunswick, Hannibal, Liberty, Moberly, Norborne, Orrick and St. Louis (3 cold storage warehouses).
NEBRASKA: Cozad, Elm Creek, Hastings, Lexington, Odessa, Omaha, Platte River, Schuyler and Willow Island.
OKLAHOMA: Shawnee.
TENNESSEE: Memphis.

Christmas and Giving Back

Chapter 15

The W. J. Small Company grew fast through the depression years. Hundreds of people worked for the company during the mid-1930s. They worked very hard and still struggled to feed and clothe themselves. In appreciation, W. J. and his wife, Hazel, began hosting Christmas parties for employees and their children.

The first parties were held at Smalls' home on the front lawn. Celebrating began with the lighting of a big cedar tree at the corner of their yard. Everyone sang Christmas carols, and Hazel and W. J. passed out bags of fruit and candy to the children.

As the company grew, invitations were extended through local newspapers to all grade school children and their little sisters and brothers not old enough to go to school. Later, the invitations stretched "to every child in the vicinity." Further newspaper announcements were published the day before the party. The first invitations were signed, "Your loving Santa Claus," or, "Your loving Mr. and Mrs. Santa Claus." The parties began at 7 p.m. on Christmas Eve.

As the Christmas parties got bigger, they were held at different company locations. There were no parties during the war, but after the war they were held at Neodesha High School; invitations went out to "everyone in Neodesha and surrounding communities." Programs were provided by school children, and later, by entertainers brought in from other towns.

After the war, the community Christmas celebrations were held a few days before Christmas rather than on Christmas Eve. By this time, W. J.'s and Hazel's family had grown, and they entertained 20 to 30 family members at their home on Christmas

SANTA CLAUS WILL BE HERE CHRISTMAS EVE.

Mr. and Mrs. Santa Claus Will Attend Mr. and Mrs. W. J. Small's Christmas Party.

Santa Will Have Treats For All the Children.

The Time and Date, 7:30 P. M., Next Wednesday—The Place, the W. J. Small Home on South Fourth Street.

Northland, Dec. 16, 1941. My Dear Children of Neodesha: Well, well, it's Christmas time again—almost time for us to come. We are very busy in our workshop with patterns, tools and paint pots putting the last touch on gifts for girls and boys.

On Christmas Eve we'll glide thru the sky. Our reindeers are fleet and it's a long way, but we'll be there on time. We hope you will all be at the Small home to greet us.

We will be at the Christmas party that Mr. and Mrs. W. J. Small are giving to all grade school girls and boys and their little sisters and brothers who are not old enough to go to school. This party is to be held in Small's yard on South Fourth street under the big lighted Christmas tree. We'll be looking for you.

Be sure to meet us at 7:30 o'clock next Wednesday night, December 24. Chuckling with glee, we will have a nice treat for you and then back we must dash, for Santa's list is long and there are others we must see.

Your loving, MR. AND MRS. SANTA CLAUS.

Eve with dinner and gifts.

In 1948, the town party was held in the high school auditorium. Entertainment included a movie, magician's act and, of course, Santa Claus, who joined his "helpers" to hand out about 1,000 bags of fruit and candy. Arrangements for this and later parties were made by the Neodesha Lions Club.

The parties got bigger each year. Invitations by the newspaper covered two full pages, and by 1951 and 1952, 2,000 to 3,000 people attended.

For the parties, Hazel and a crew of helpers from the family and company made the bags of candy and fruit. Hazel set up large tables in the basement of their home, and friends and family formed a production line to put them together. The bags would go down the line – one person would add an apple, the next, an orange, then another would throw in different types of hard candy.

Hazel ordered the candy and bags through a local grocery store, Johnnie Moore's IGA. In the beginning there were 200 bags of candy to fill; by 1952, there were 3,000. Every child and adult in town received a bag filled with candy. Bags were also distributed to local nursing homes, hospitals and disabled individuals.

OTHER GIVING

W. J. and Hazel Small gave time, love, work and money back to their communities' churches, hospitals, Scouts, schools and needy families wherever they went. W. J. contributed to the educations of not only his family members, but to those of many of his employees as well. In addition to school aid, he was especially supportive of religious affiliations and hospitals. Kathleen, his sister-in-law, often said that W. J. wrote checks of donation each month to "a list as long as your arm."

In August in later years, Hazel personally bought school clothes for many children, and helped pay hospital

Mr., Mrs. Santa Claus Hosts to Community Party Saturday Night

More Than 2,000 Persons Turn Out To Party Around Huge Xmas Tree

Over 2,000 Neodeshans turned out Saturday night to see Mr. and Mrs. Santa Claus at Mr. and Mrs. W. J. Small's annual Christmas party at the high school gymnasium. Arrangements for the big affair were under the direction of the Neodesha Lions club.

Santa and his wife entertained the crowd by singing a duet, "Winter Wonderland". Santa's solo was "Rudolph, the Red Nosed Reindeer" and Mrs. Santa sang "Frosty, the Snowman."

Huge Tree

One of the main attractions was the huge Christmas tree decorated with over 500 lights. Every child was greeted by Mr. or Mrs. Santa and their helpers and was given a large sack of candy.

A Christmas film, "Santa and the Fairy Queen," was shown and a community sing was under the direction of Bueford Roper. Accordion selections were played by Mrs. Ethel Beals.

and medical bills for young people with special problems. Both W. J. and Hazel were willing to give back for their own special fortunes.

The following are paragraphs from an anonymous letter written years after the Smalls moved from Neodesha.

No memory of "The Spirit of Christmas Past" in Neodesha would be complete without thinking of the Christmas parties given for the town by W. J. Small and his wife.

I often think of those occasions during this time of the year, probably because of the profound effect they have had on my view of what life in a mid-western town was, could be, and might be today if we took the time to work on it.

...My earliest memory of those Christmas occasions is that they were held in front of his house on Fourth Street.

...I can remember everyone gathering in front of the house, there would be a great deal of carol singing, then Mr. and Mrs. Small would introduce Santa Claus (Howard Simpson never seemed to be able to make the parties). There would be sacks of candy for everyone, then the Smalls would turn on their Christmas lights.

The lighting of the lights would be followed by some more carols, a local minister would say something about the meaning of Christmas, and we would all go home to feel good about living in Neodesha.

Later on, as the popularity of the parties grew, the yard of the Smalls' house became too (pardon the expression) small for the crowds. The last few I remember being held were at the high school, in the gymnasium. By then, however, they had become major productions with entertainment.

To
Our old
customers
.... our old
Holiday   friends   of   Greetings
years   standing
and .... to our
newer   customers,
who   in   the   course
of   coming   years   we
hope   will   become   old
customers and old friends.
.... To all whose friendship
and good will have helped to
make our Christmas more thoroughly
enjoyable,   we say thank you ....
Thank you sincerely and heartily ...
We wish you a real MERRY CHRISTMAS and a
Bright, Happy and Prosperous New Year.

.   .
.   .
.   .

The W. J. Small Company

Neodesha, Kansas

Epilogue

W. J. Small didn't retire after selling the company to Archer-Daniels-Midland. He had been to Arizona a few times, and in raising and dehydrating some alfalfa there, he saw the need and possibilities for irrigating the dessert.

THE REST OF THE STORY

W. J. bought dessert land around Scottsdale and Mesa, near Phoenix, and drilled it for water. He tried to get just about anybody he could to work for him in Arizona but was hard pressed to convince former employees in Kansas that they would be doing the right thing by moving to the hot, dry dessert. Offering to resell land "real cheap" to a Kansas employee, Johnny Clifton, if Johnny would come to work for him there, W. J. said, "you'll be well off in ten or fifteen years." Johnny wasn't sure, but said he thought W. J. had only paid $5 or $10 an acre for this barren dessert land. Johnny could not move his wife and children to Arizona where they would have to travel 35 miles to schools. However, he continued to work for W. J. from Kansas.

W. J. bought a bulldozer and tractors in Kansas and had them trucked to Arizona to level dessert and drill wells for irrigation. Clifton and W. J.'s brother, Elmer, obtained 16-cylinder engines from World War II PT boats, customized them, built bases for them and sent them to W. J. He used them for generating electricity for pumping well water in the dessert.

W. J. went on to buy more dessert land, some of which was in cantaloupes, watermelon and grapes. This land was in or near the resort city of Scottsdale which then had dirt roads and a population of about 10,000. Scottsdale had obtained "City" status only three years earlier in 1961. W. J. and Hazel settled in Phoenix, and W. J. continued his involvement with developing real estate until they both passed away in 1981. W. J. was 94.

SELECTED BIBLIOGRAPHY

This book was researched and assembled through a combination of printed research materials and interviews with key family members and employees of the W. J. Small Company:

Interviews
Bob Blackwell, 2/99 & 8/04.
Marie Clegg with Gene O'Dell and Roy Failor, 5/01.
Roy Failor, Gene O'Dell & Rollin Vandever, 6/99.
Adrin Small, 5/01.
Kathleen Small, 6/99.
Elmer Small, 6/99.
Rollin Vandever, 12/96, 1/97, 3/97, 8/98, 11/01.
Vera Wagar with Frank & Gertrude (Gertie) Wagar.

Speech Sources
Richard L. Kathe, Executive Vice President, American Dehydrators Association, at 25th Anniversary Convention, Scottsdale, AZ, January 24-29, 1966.

Book Sources
Neodesha Centennial Committee, *Little Bear Tracks*, Neodesha Printing Co., 1971.
Goodhue, L.D., "Vitamins" *After A Hundred Years, The Yearbook of Agriculture 1962,* The United States Government Printing Office.
Goodhue, L.D., "DDT" *After A Hundred Years, The Yearbook of Agriculture 1962,* The United States Government Printing Office.
Jennings, Peter and Brewster, Todd, *The Century*, New York: Doubleday, 1998.
Shinn, Rodger, *Square Deal*, Fredonia, Kansas.
Klinkenbourg, Verlin, *Making Hay*, New York: Vintage Departures, Vintage Books, A Division of Random House, 1987.

Internet Sources
"Alfalfa," Herbal Information Center, http://www.primary.net/~gic/herb/alfalfa.htm
Shaw, Vicki, "Alfalfa," Hodgson Field Crops Student Work, http://agri.atu.edu
USDA Agriculture Research Service, http://www.ars.usda.gov/
"The Rector and Visitors of the University of Virginia," Miller Center of Public Affairs, http://www.American President.org
Agriculture in the Classroom, USDA, http://www.agclassroom.org/
Wessels Living History Farm, http://www.livinghistoryfarm.org/

Newspaper Sources
Most of the newspaper articles listed were archived as clippings by Hazel Small over the years, and as such, exact publication dates, or even which newspaper they appeared in is not always known. Some are at the Neodesha, Kansas, History Museum.
Neodesha Register
"Obituary of J. B. Small." 1/19/22.
"Lions and Their Wives Royally Entertained" 11/25/26.

"Has Become One of Neodesha's Largest Industries" 11/4/27.

"Purchase of Louisiana Ice Service" 12/30/32.

"W. J. Small Hay Co. Buys Second Dehydrating Unit" 10/1/34.

"Installs Dehydrating Units In Two New Fields" 4/6/36.

"Encourages Alfalfa Growing" 1937.

"Banks to be Consolidated" 1/21/38.

"Neodesha's Two Banks to be Merged" 1/27/38.

"Small Company More Than Doubles Investment Here" 4/16/38.

"One of Neodesha's Most Valuable Industries" 4/21/38.

"Jack Pitney Joins Small Company Staff" 2/2/40.

"(W. J. Small) Escapes Serious Injury in Car Accident" 2/5/40.

"History of the W. J. Small Company" 4/1/40.

"K-State Group Visits Small Co. Plant" 4/29/40.

"Dismisses Charges Against W. J. Small" 6/8/40.

"...established a plant near Liberty" 12/29/40.

"H. E. Osburn and Paul Dice go to Liberty, Missouri" 12/40.

"The W. J. Small Co. Organizes New Company" 1/1/41.

"W. J. Small Organizes a New Company" 1/2/41.

"Annual Meeting of the W. J. Small Co., Inc." 1/13/41.

"New Neodesha Industry Now in Operation" 1/22/41.

"Small Co. Expands Its Facilities in the South" 1/31/41.

"Dale Kenyon Resigns Position with Gas Co." 2/7/41.

"Dehydrator Plant Begins Operation Monday Morning" 5/23/41.

"Large Hay Barn Destroyed By Fire" 10/22/41.

"Neodesha Obtains New National Defense Plant" 5/5/42.

"Newest Industry Expands Rapidly In War Production" 5/11/42.

"Growing Pains Experienced by Neodesha's New War Industry" 5/14/42.

"New Plant Here Moving Toward Full Production" 5/42.

"W. J. Small and Associates Acquire Ice Service Company" 6/4/42.

"Rapid Expansion Marks First Year of METCO in Neodesha" 3/18/43.

"No Alfalfa Marketed Here This Spring" 4/27/44.

"The W. J. Small Co. Suffers Heavy Loss at Brunswick, Mo." 10/28/44.

"Add Three New Employees and More New Equipment" 3/15/45.

"Fly DDT to Polio Area" 5/17/45.

"First Carload of DDT Left Neodesha Monday" 6/14/45.

"Midwest Engineering and Tool Co." 6/14/45.

"Explosion and Fire Destroy Laboratory" 6/28/45.

"City's Newest Industry Topic of rotary Program" 7/21/45.

"More Thrilling News for Neodesha" 8/45.

"The W. J. Small Companies in Spotlight" 9/45.

"Our Newest Industry Hits (KC) Stars Feature Page" 1945.

"Neodeshan President Dehydrators Association" 1/46.

"Casserly Joins Small Company" 1/29/46.

"Judge Bradfield Resigns After 5 Years with District" 2/7/46.

"Repeat of Kansas City story re Building in KC" 8/1/46.

"Public thank you from W. J. Small" 1946.

"Smalls to Furnish New Hospital Nursery" 1/11/47.

"First National Bank's 75th Birthday Today" 1/16/47.

"Smalls Donate $2,000 for Use At Hospital Here" 2/14/47.

"Most Destructive Fire in Several Years" 9/25/47.

"Six-Million Dollar..." 1/8/48

"Lightning Sets Warehouse Afire This Morning" 10/6/48.

"Airosol, Inc. To Nebraska Firm" 11/1/48.

"W. J. Small Co. Suffers Flood Loss of $300,000" 7/26/51.

"Archer-Daniels Buys Meal Firm" 8/30/51.

"The W. J. Small Co., Bought by Archer-Daniels-Midland Co." 8/30/51.

"Small Company Acquires Colorado Milling Concern" Exact date unknown.

"Neodesha's War Production Plant Expands" (METCO) Exact date unknown.

"Small's Big Hay Barn Burned Last Night" (Fredonia) Exact date unknown.

"METCO Manufacturing DDT Insecticide Here" Exact date unknown.

"W. J. Small States His Views" Exact date unknown.

"Public Thank You for helping fight fire" Exact date unknown.

Independence Reporter

"Independence to Have Dehydrating Plant" 1/11/40.

"Girl Scout Council Holds Annual Dinner" 1/47.

"Small Alfalfa Mill Storage Burns Today" 10/6/48.

"Elk Valley Alfalfa Mills, Inc." Exact date unknown.

Kansas City Star

"Small Company Expands Kansas City Plant" 1/5/39.

"An Alfalfa Plant Expands" 1/5/39.

"An Industry from Idea – Small Town Banker No Longer" 1/8/39.

"A Vigorous Infant Industry Enlivens Small Kansas Town" 7/29/45.

"Neodesha's New Industry Attracting Wide Attention" 8/2/45.

"Scientists and Businessmen Gather To View Midwest's Progress in Research" 12/3/45.

"W. J. Small Buys 6-Story Building in Kansas City" 8/8/46.

"Camera Catches a Falling Wall" (Neodesha warehouse fire) 10/2/48.

"At the Midwest Research Institute Meeting" 12/9/47.

"Six-Million Dollar Kansas Corporation Headed by Small" 1/6/48.

El Dorado Times

"Small Business." 9/1/38.

"Alfalfa Dehydrating Plant for El Dorado" 7/9/43.

"Alfalfa Plant Locates Here" 7/43.

"An Acquisition of Great Worth" 7/43.

The Brunswicker

"Alfalfa Mill to Locate Here" 1939.

Boonville Daily News

"Work Started on Huge Alfalfa Dehydration Unit by W. J. Small Co." 3/18/41.

World-Herald

"States Alfalfa Even Keeps Turkeys from Fighting; It Has the Vitamins" 9/21/46.

"ADM Grain Firm Buys Small, Inc." 8/27/51.

Norborne Democrat

"Norborne Welcomes..." 5/23/41.

Kansas City Kansan

"See Bright Future in Alfalfa Plant Here" 10/11/1935.

Lexington Clipper

"Alfalfa!" 1914.

Wichita Eagle

"Article on Belle Plaine plant" 7/12/40.

Mt. Hope Clarion
"Caple, Orville" 7/12/40.

Minneapolis Morning Tribune
"Archer-Daniels-Midland Reports Net Worth Reaches Record High" 8/27/51.

Minneapolis Star
"A-D-M Firm Assets Hit Record Peak" 8/27/51.

Wall Street Journal
"Archer-Daniels-Midland Buys W. J. Small Co., Alfalfa Meal Producer" 8/27/51.

Unidentified Newspapers
"Dehydrators are Having Busy Run" Lawrence, KS. 4/15/39.
"New Mill in Fairfax District" Kansas City. 12/31/39.
"Power Service to Dehydrating Plant" Lexington, MO. 5/3/40.
"Indictment Against W. J. Small dismissed by Judge Hopkins" Kansas City. 6/8/40.
"Alfalfa Mill Proves Boon to Farmers" Belle Plaine, KS. 7/12/40.
"New Dehydrating Unit which is Today Making Farm and Factory Closer" Belle Plaine, KS. 7/12/40.
"You Can't Do It, – It's Done" Decatur, IL. 6/19/41.
"Alfalfa Plant May Come Here In Permanance" Abilene, KS. 9/23/41.
"Abilene May Be Site of Alfalfa Dehyddrating Co." Abilene, KS. 9/24/41.
"Lions Get All Angles on New Alfalfa Plant" Abilene, KS. 9/30/41.
"Start on New Alfalfa Dehydrating Plant" Marion, KS. 7/1/42.
"Alfalfa Dehydrating Plant Rounds Into Shape" Marion, KS. 7/8/42.
"Large Business Deal concluded This Week by W. J. Small and Associates" Chicago, IL. 12/30/43.
"Airosol Chartered" Topeka, KS. 7/31/45.
"W. J. Small Buys Office Building in Kansas City" Kansas City. 8/1/46.
"Fire Damage at Feed Mill May Be Heavy" Decatur, IL. 1946.
"Carnival Grounds Sea of Bags" Decatur, IL. 11/10/48.
"$90,000 Warehouse Fie Still Smouldering" Decatur, IL. 11/19/48.
"Small's Will Celebrate 20th Year" Kansas City. 3/8/51.
"Small Company's Shawnee Unit Destroyed by Fire" Topeka, KS. Exact date unknown.
"Warehouse Burns In Early Morning; $125,000 Damage" Decatur, IL. Exact date unknown.
"Small Company Advertising Used by City Utilities" Kansas City. Exact date unknown.
"Still Fight A Blaze" Kansas City. Exact date unknown.
"Alfalfa Dehydration" Mt. Hope, KS. Exact date unknown.
"Dehydrating Plant is at Work..." Excelsior Springs, Mo. Exact date unknown.
"Hannibal's Newest Industry Begins Operation" Hannibal, MO. Exact date unknown.

Other Print Sources
"W. J. Small Shipper of Prairie and Alfalfa Hay"; and "W. J. Small Dealer in Alfalfa and Prairie Hay, " Printed Business Forms, 1922.
W. J. Small Letter to American Dehydrator's Association, 12/29/65.
W. J. Small Affidavit for the IRS (no date), in possession of Bob Blackwell, Trustee for W. J. and Hazel Small.